OPINION AND KNOWLEDGE

Bernárdez: The idea that the sum of opinions is truth is a monstrous thing. By this criterion, as Christ was crucified by a vote, the conclusion would be that it was a good act, instead of a monstrosity. The fact that everyone believes a certain thing means absolutely nothing.

Borges: What seems strange to me is that everyone can pronounce on politics but is not allowed to do so in philosophy, mathematics or science . . .

Bernárdez: There is no doubt that wisdom, in the great epochs, was of an initiatory character, something not sold in the market. It has to have, in the first place, conditions for receiving and being given it . . .

Borges: Now, in contrast, it is assumed that ignorance is meritorious . . . We are heirs to all the Western tradition and to what we can acquire of the Eastern as well.

— Dialogue between Jorge Luis Borges and Francisco Luiz Bernárdez, **La Nacion**, Buenos Aires, 24 November 1974.

£3.50

JORGE LUIS BÓRGES:
SOURCES AND ILLUMINATION

JORGE LUIS BORGES

Titles in English translation.

THE ALEPH & OTHER STORIES

BORGES ON WRITING

DOCTOR BRODIE'S REPORT

DREAMTIGERS

FICTIONS

IN PRAISE OF DARKNESS

INTRODUCTION TO AMERICAN LITERATURE

LABYRINTHS: SELECTED STORIES & OTHER
WRITINGS

OTHER INQUISITIONS

A PERSONAL ANTHOLOGY

A UNIVERSAL HISTORY OF INFAMY

EXTRAORDINARY TALES
by Borges & A. B. Casares

THE BOOK OF IMAGINARY BEINGS
by Borges & M. Guerrero

AN INTRODUCTION TO ENGLISH LITERATURE
by Borges & Maria Esther Vazquez

JORGE LUIS BORGES:
SOURCES AND ILLUMINATION

by
Professor Giovanna de Garayalde

THE OCTAGON PRESS
LONDON

First Published 1978

© by The Octagon Press

ISBN 900 860 61 8

Printed in Great Britain by
Tonbridge Printers Ltd, Tonbridge, Kent.

CONTENTS

NOTE

This book contains a number of quotations from the works of Borges and of Idries Shah and from critical writings about Borges. A list of books referred to is given below; the abbreviated title shown in brackets is that used for references in the text. Wherever there is a published English translation of a text originally in Spanish, this has been cited, but it should be noted that the translation used here is not necessarily identical with the published version. A full bibliography is given at the end of the book.

Ana María Barrenechea	Borges, the Labyrinth Maker (*Labyrinth*)
Jorge Luís Borges	The Aleph and Other Stories, 1933–69 (*Aleph*)
	El Aleph (1949) (*El Aleph*)
	Cuentos Breves y Extraordinarios (*Cuentos*)
	Discusión (*Discusión*)
	Dreamtigers (*Dreamtigers*)
	Fictions (*Fictions*)
	Historia de la Eternidad (*Eternidad*)
	In Praise of Darkness (*Darkness*)
	Other Inquisitions, 1937–52 (*Inquisitions*)
	A Personal Anthology (*Anthology*)
	A Universal History of Infamy (*Infamy*)
Luís Harss and Barbara Dohmann	Into the Mainstream (*Mainstream*)
Alicia Jurado	Genio y Figura de Jorge Luís Borges (*Genio*)
Idries Shah	Caravan of Dreams (*Caravan*)
	The Magic Monastery (*Monastery*)
	Reflections (*Reflections*)
	The Sufis (*Sufis*)
	Tales of the Dervishes (*Dervishes*)
	Thinkers of the East (*Thinkers*)
	The Way of the Sufi (*Way*)
	Wisdom of the Idiots (*Wisdom*)

I
Borges: A Mysterious and Unknown Personality

ㅍㅍㅍㅍㅍㅍㅍㅍㅍㅍㅍㅍㅍㅍㅍㅍㅍㅍㅍㅍㅍㅍㅍㅍㅍㅍㅍㅍ

His name is Jorge Luís Borges; he is an Argentine and lives in Buenos Aires. In 1961 he shared the Publishers' International Prize with Samuel Becket. His reputation is still the subject of much controversy in Argentina. Some questionable admirers have praised him for the best-known and least significant part of his work; the nationalists have accused him of being unpatriotic and an Anglophile, the left, of hating the working classes, the youth in general, of not being in tune with present day problems. Most people have judged him cold and cerebral. Everyone without exception has been angered, at one time or another, by his press statements.

What is an undoubted fact is that the author is scrupulously disguised in his works. Strangely enough a foreigner, the Chilean Luís Harss, has probably understood this aspect of Borges' personality better than anyone else. In a book published in English and called *Into the Mainstream*, he says:

'To a large extent the fascinating effect of Borges' writing is achieved through the expert use of bibliographical references that hint at meanings that are never quite revealed. He himself writes: "The solution to the mystery is always inferior to the mystery itself. This principle has been used as the basis for one of our most effective literary methods".

'Ignorance and malice are resolved to distort Borges. He is a great joker and his pranks usually upset people. He takes pleasure in seeming ingenious and contradictory. Occasionally, when pressed by some untimely interviewer, he offends by improvising words or principles. He is a master of insinuation. He annoyed everyone four or five years ago when he flatly refused to attend a conference of writers in Buenos Aires because, he said, it was

7

costing the bankrupt government too much money. He joined the Conservative Party not long ago because of his "scepticism", as he later frankly explained, for as he once said, "Politics are a form of tedium". However he has recently spent his time in writing statements against Castro. On various occasions he has declared himself anti-Nazi, anti-Communist and anti-Christian. A short while back he made fools of people in Venezuela where, during a speech delivered in the presence of literary personalities who expected to hear a flow of praises for the local writers, he talked about Walt Whitman. He is not at all impressed by the supporters of the native literature; according to him, "There are no Indians on the River Plate".

'He is an absent-minded lecturer – clubs and literary circles are after him day and night; they carry him off in a taxi from wherever he may be in the city. He will drop the subject in the middle of a sentence and, intimidated by his audience, digress, always in a most obliging manner, on the mysteries of some obscure etymology, or shock the patriotic audience by maintaining, always most politely, that the poetry of the "gauchos" is an invention of the writers, that football was imported from England, or that the idolized Carlos Gardel was French.' (*Mainstream*, pp. 121, 104, 105)

In actual fact, I have verified through my everyday experience as a teacher of literature that, though Borges is often mentioned by my colleagues and pupils, generally speaking the largest and most significant part of his work is unknown. Literary critics in general have classified him in the 'fantastic tales' category. Many people have tried to puzzle out the philosophical or theological basis that appears to underlie his exotic themes and countless learned quotations. The results have been somewhat confusing. The number of influences that have been traced in Borges' work is overwhelming.

A complete if rather condensed summary of literary criticism of Borges' work is to be found in *Historia de la Literatura Argentina*, edited by Adolfo Prieto. The following are the conclusions drawn regarding his philosophy:

'From an ideological point of view, Borges' conception of history and reality amounts to a frozen and futureless destiny. Borges is

8

rejecting History when he postulates the cyclic repetition of time, which means that it is impossible for a man to create new possibilities. The idea of the eternal return is not just a paradox; it is the denial of progress, the most forthright denial of man's originality. By denying that the possibility of objectively understanding reality exists, Borges is also denying man the possibility of changing that reality. If our actions are reflexes of other actions that could have taken place a thousand years ago, our will, our reasons for doing things and our intention of justifying a whole lifetime are senseless. Denial of the special features of each life, denial of the possibilities of influencing reality, denial of the meaning of our destiny and the universe: in other words, denial of rationality and history; poetic irrationalism that rejects two of the most human and optimistic principles of man.

'The question that seems to arise is this: Is the aesthetic wonder, the creation of outstanding prose and a rich and fantastic universe sufficient to justify this ideology, which freezes us and condemns us to impossibility and irrationality?' (p. 1139)

II

A Foreshadowing of Borges' Thought in the Ancient Middle East

When I first consulted the biography that traces the philosophical content of Borges' work, I was most surprised to discover that what was, to my mind, the principal and most direct influence on him was not emphasized. I was even more sure that my conviction was correct when, a short time ago, I came across certain definite facts. I venture to maintain my theory because I believe that two chance circumstances have helped me in my work and have rendered my position different from that of his previous critics. First, I had come into contact with Sufi literature and second, as a consequence I have approached the problem from the opposite direction. I am sure that had I started from Borges' works, I should have been confused by the large amount of apparently unconnected data. However, quite unintentionally, I first came across what I believe were his sources and then later recognized these in his work. During my youth I had the opportunity of reading Eastern literature and meeting with people who had certain links with the East. This enabled me to glimpse a world that is generally unknown or misinterpreted in the West: the world of the anonymous and solitary mystics who, after a long inner journey, arrive at a higher wisdom. This wisdom is totally inaccessible to the Western mentality. For this reason the West had relegated it to the inferior level of magic and is only now trying to study some of its outward manifestations in a scientific manner.

In my opinion these esoteric ways coincided with the metaphysical search contained in Borges' writings. The constant references throughout Borges' books to Eastern places, personalities and writers and the coincidences in his approach to themes such as time, reality, destiny, the infinite, etc., were to my mind all

11

very significant. But my conviction would never have gone beyond the subjective plane of mere personal opinion had I not made contact with Sufism. Towards the end of 1972, the International Exhibition of the Sufi Book was held in Buenos Aires. The exhibition covered part of this literature, produced over a period of fifteen centuries: a hundred books in various Western languages. Evidently a movement had begun, aimed at diffusion of this knowledge within our culture and from authentic sources.

In one of the books, Idries Shah's *Tales of the Dervishes*, I found various tales which I had read in Borges' books. This coincidence intrigued me and I started looking for others. I found so many and so much concrete bibliographical data, that I could not but conclude that there was a foreshadowing of Borges' thought in Sufi thought. Generally speaking, Borges' critics have been divided into detractors – who say his work is destructive or useless, a superfluous luxury that forgets man and is satisfied with empty patterns of reality while there are immediate problems requiring urgent attention – or admirers – who try to justify him by attributing to him the doctrines that he expounds in his works.

If I am seeking to establish a link between the author and Sufism, my intention is not to affiliate him to Sufism nor to show a conscious attitude on his part, but simply to establish points in common between Borges' writing and this teaching – which is seemingly just as disturbing – in order the better to understand this mysterious man by drawing an analogy between him and Sufism. In this way we shall be able to show that as a writer he fulfils his obligations towards his contemporaries.

It is however extremely difficult, in view of the type of literature involved, to transform into a theoretical essay what has been for me personally a direct and untransferable experience. Explaining Borges through Sufism runs into difficulties which are inherent in the understanding of Sufism, which is so far removed from our way of thinking and which has baffled both Western investigators and translators. The most conflicting definitions have turned it into the least understood Eastern teaching, despite the fact that it is one of those that has the greatest links with our culture because of its diffusion in Medieval Saracendom and the fact that the Arabs remained in Spain for eight centuries. However, the desire of the Sufis to divulge their teaching openly in the West for the first time after many centuries of silence has safeguarded that teaching from much of the reigning confusion and many mistaken ideas. To achieve this, they have made certain statements which are quite exceptional for this type of teaching and which have helped to clarify the real meaning of their literature. These statements have also thrown light upon the meaning of Borges' writings.

When one takes the first steps in approaching Sufism, one comes up against statements such as that the Sufis are 'independent of all philosophical or religious doctrines', despite the fact that they have produced the greatest mystics of Islam, and that they frequently refer to Moses, Jesus or Mohammed as Teachers of the Way. They also maintain that they have influenced the works of St John of the Cross, St Teresa, St Francis of Assisi, Bacon, Dante, Shakespeare and Raymond Lully among others. These assertions are documented in the works of famous and neutral investigators belonging to our culture, such as for example the Spanish professor, Asín Palacios.

The great Sufi teachers seem to have had the most widely varying occupations: some led a monastic life and others a worldly one; there have been scientists, investigators, musicians, poets and artisans. Sometimes they were considered saints and at other times heretics. Their teaching seems different through the ages. They often had opposing political, philosophical or religious views during the same period.

How can such heterogeneous elements be connected by means of a single common factor, which is Sufism? Our Western minds are confused since this has no precedents within the fixed patterns of our culture. As one becomes familiar with their literature and the explanations that accompany it, the picture becomes slightly clearer. I will try to give a summary of the principles of this teaching, which has no doctrines of any kind, in order to establish a connection with Borges' works which may enable us to understand the inner content of this writer's enigmatic writings.

The Sufis maintain that man, like all living beings, is included in a continual and evolutionary process within the Universe. It is man's duty to take part harmoniously in this process and to participate in the advancement of this evolution. But because of his way of seeing things, he can only become partially aware of the process. His perceptions are faulty because they are subjective and relative and are conditioned by the outside world; therefore man interprets things according to limited patterns that are not objective and consequently he has little capacity for judging things correctly.

The most complex interrelation of cause and effect that would explain reality cannot be transcribed into the language of the mind in its present state.

'What we take to be reality is really more primitive short-term rule of thumb. For example, we tend to look at events one-sidedly. We also assume, without any justification, that an event happens as it were in a vacuum. In actual fact, all events are associated with all other events. . . . If you look at any action which you do, or which anyone else does, you will find that it was prompted by one of many possible stimuli; and also that it is never an isolated action – it has consequences, many of them ones which you would never expect, certainly which you could not have planned. . . . It is only when we are ready to experience our inter-relation with the organism of life that we can appreciate mystical experience. That is to say a direct and total perception of truth.' (*Sufis*, p. 71)

Meanwhile man is in a state that is called 'a dream'. Therefore he must 'awaken', but this is not to be achieved through academic effort nor by exercising the intellect. Reality has elements that are beyond the reach of rationalism; the only way to encompass it is through direct or intuitive perception of truth. But man must first achieve a different and far wider working of his mind.

In one way or another certain people throughout history have become aware of the inner meaning of life. These people have always provided the necessary means for other people to reach understanding and self-realization. The Sufis have been among these people for over a thousand years. But their teaching differs from all those known to us in that it cannot be imparted in a general and theoretical way, nor by a prescribed course of study which is the same for all students. Sufi knowledge, they say, cannot be given to a disciple, it is something that happens to him.

14

Since the Sufis state that man is incapable of perceiving truth at will, their objective cannot be to inculcate certain dogmas or beliefs. On the contrary, they try to establish a blueprint or model in the mind to help it to operate in another manner and to make it possible for every man to know himself and to discover his real role in life.

As far back as 1200 A.D. – and many centuries before Darwin – the poet Jalaludin Rumi maintained that man was a product of evolution and that his new organs came into being as a result of necessity. Basing themselves on this principle, the Sufis try to 'awaken' or activate an organ of higher perception, through the development of inner (mystic) forces that are inherent in man, that is to say by conscious evolution.

When man achieves his fullest development he possesses extraordinary powers, which both Eastern and Western occultism aspire to. Sufi literature describes these miraculous faculties in their mystical teachers, for example the annihilation of conventional time. They explain, however, that when these things occur, they are simply the application of laws of nature that have not yet been recognized and correctly understood by orthodox science, just as not so long ago hypnosis and telepathy were not recognized either.

'The sixth sense which the Sufi acquires, which is assumed by theoreticians to be a sense of complete prescience, of almost divine all-knowledge, is nothing of the kind. Like all the other senses it has its limitations. Its function is not to make the Perfected Man all-wise, but to enable him to fulfil a mission of greater perception and fuller life. He no longer suffers from the sense of uncertainty and incompleteness which is familiar to other people.' (*Sufis*, p. 81)

There are precise techniques to free the mind from preconceptions and conditioned ideas, as well as to stimulate the working of mental forces that are not normally used. Many of these techniques are to be found in Sufi literary works: tales, fables, poems, sayings, etc. The language is conventional and symbolic. They do not use the literal meaning only, because they deny that words – which are merely a reflection of a rational and abstract concept – can convey the whole multifaceted range of vital reality. The historical and religious content and the form of the saying thus simply provide the structure for manipulated and enciphered

material which can produce an effect on the reader similar to that
of a kaleidoscope, that is to say it is projected at various levels,
according to the situation of the reader and the place and time
of the reading. Only a symbol can have such flexibility of
expression.

The context generally refers to psychological processes rather
than to historical events or moral conclusions that are evident
on the surface. Far from wishing to convey theoretical truths, the
object of the content is effectiveness and the ability to produce,
through a vital impact, an inner transformation in the disciple
and to set in motion real development. Since Sufi teaching is
based on the concept of essence rather than the concept of God,
it may or may not have a religious context, but whatever the
context, it is simply a vehicle to improve the human mind and
has no end in itself. The context has metaphorical and practical
characteristics and is not meant to convey dogmatic truths. The
Sufis use words such as God, demon, heaven, hell, angels, but in a
technical and figurative sense, which differs from the use made of
these words by religions in general. 'Angels are the powers hidden
in the faculties and organs of man', according to Ibn el-Arabi,
one of the greatest Sufi teachers. Hell and paradise also have
another meaning:

'The Sufi is he who neither fears hell nor covets paradise.'

(*Way*, p. 45)

'In cell and cloister, in monastery and synagogue,
Some fear hell and others dream of Paradise.
But no man who really knows the secrets of his God
Has planted seeds like these within his heart.'   (*Way*, p. 33)

Through the ages the Sufi sages have adapted their formulations
to the specific needs of each place, time and group of people, in
order to maintain their effectiveness and to avoid becoming a
mere repetition of basically rigid postulates. The Sufis assert that
their teaching has existed for centuries, passed on by the ancient
sages like Jesus, Moses and Mohammed, although it has been
altered and used in a lesser and inefficient way, with emphasis repeatedly placed on the literal meaning of things that are figurative
and that belong to a certain time and place. When man goes
beyond externals, he can see that all religious formulations, though

they are apparently so numerous, have the same basis, and that at this level there is no place for rituals and dogmas.

Essentially religion has two roles. The first is to organize man in a peaceful, just and safe manner, to establish and help maintain communities. The second is the inward aspect, which leads people from the outer stabilization to the performance which awakens them and helps to make them permanent. Numerous systems continue to float around in the world but virtually all are devoid of value in this inner sense, though they may not be without historical interest.

Sufism tries to create an atmosphere without the fixed rules or dogmas that can condition the disciple, in order that his behaviour should not be a mechanical projection of external stimuli. The disciple has to acquire absolute ethics based on criteria of real constructiveness and destructiveness, both for himself and for his society, and not on the threat of punishment or the promise of reward. Thus there is nothing which the disciple can lean on for guidance of a support-therapy nature.

This explains why Sufis are able to hold different political, religious or social views. Their objective, which is essential to all humanity, goes beyond those differences that separate most men.

There are, however, certain conditions that the disciple must comply with. The would-be disciple must be in the World but not of the World, that is to say he must co-exist harmoniously in the society to which he happens to belong but he must be free of all worldly ties that condition and limit his development. In order to achieve real development, he has to detach himself from personal, material things. But he cannot withdraw from the world, like an ascetic, because if he did this he would be separating himself from reality and avoiding his duty as a human being.

The Sufi is destined to a social life. It is of fundamental importance that he should dedicate his life to a useful occupation; his aim is to be an ideal member of society. In this way, he is serving the infinite, himself and society. But these conditions are not ethical objectives in themselves, nor religious precepts; they are the method to free man from the one-sided and subjective approach to which he is limited by his personal interests.

'Because the average person thinks in patterns and cannot

accommodate himself to a really different point of view, he loses a great deal of the meaning of life. He may live, even progress, but he cannot understand all that is going on.' (*Sufis*, p. 59)

The Sufis assert that the present diffusion of this teaching is due to humanity's current need for normal development. To quote Idries Shah[1], the greatest living authority on Sufism, he is interested in making available in the West those aspects of Sufism that will be of use to the West. The Sufis use a new point of view in order to overcome the conditioning which our materialistic society has imposed. Our ills are due mainly to the one-sided rationalism of our culture and the loss of the intuitive faculty that would have enabled us to gain access to an area of knowledge which cannot be reached through the intellectual mechanism. They believe that for the first time in history conscious evolution has ceased to be a choice open to man and has become a necessity on which our future depends.

This teaching tries to join the spiritual plane, generally represented by religions, to the scientific one. It is not based on dogmas but on objective knowledge, experienced through the Sufi tradition and resulting from the application of certain laws of nature that are adapted to the specific needs of each time and place, application which requires direct observation, the renewed analysis of the circumstances and practical verification.

---

[1] Idries Shah is a member of an Afghan family descended from Mohammed. He now lives partly in England, where he is Director of Studies of the Institute for Cultural Research. Apart from his literary work, Idries Shah has specialized in various scientific fields related to the problems of man in the twentieth century and his immediate future from an ecological point of view. Cf. *Who's Who In the Arab World*, Beirut, 1971–73, p. 1493; and Professor L. F. Rushbrook Williams (editor) *Sufi Studies: East and West*, New York 1973 and London 1974.

III
Guide-lines of Borges' Thought

The purpose of this monograph is not to reveal and then prove the existence of unnoticed guide-lines in Borges' writings since, in broad outline, I agree with his two most authorized critics: Ana María Barrenechea and Alicia Jurado, the latter of whom is Borges' biographer and friend. They have already performed this function in their books, *Borges, the Labyrinth Maker* and *Genio y Figura de Jorge Luis Borges*, respectively. I will limit myself for the most part to their conclusions in order to establish coincidences between Borges' thought and Sufi ideas, thus gaining not only in conciseness but also in objectivity. Since generally speaking my views coincide with those of these two authors, my task will be to enlarge on their conclusions and to clarify them.

Both authors agree that Borges has no fixed doctrine behind all the theories that abound in his books.

'We should not search for the consistent development of a metaphysical conception throughout his works, nor should we try to find a doctrine that in his opinion is the only real key to the Universe.' (*Labyrinth*, p. 144)

'The metaphysical hypotheses that he propounds in his works do not necessarily coincide with his beliefs. The proof of this is that sometimes in one and the same paragraph he offers two contrary though equally satisfactory interpretations of a single event, without choosing either. This is confirmed by the element of doubt that runs through his writings, which are strewn with maybes and perhapses, where verbs such as postulate, guess and surmise recur as if to warn us about the dangers of certainty.' (*Genio*, p. 61)

Borges knows that our perceptions are conditioned and limited and that reality cannot be explained through reason:

'The very act of perceiving and paying attention is selective. When we fix our attention or our consciousness on something, we automatically leave out what we are not interested in. What we see and hear is a result of our recollections, our fears and our cautiousness. As regards the body, unconsciousness is a necessity for physical action. And our body knows how to pronounce a difficult paragraph; can handle stairs, knots, level-crossings, cities, fast-flowing rivers and dogs; can cross a street without being killed by the traffic; knows how to beget, how to breathe, how to sleep and perhaps how to kill our body but not our intelligence. Our life is a series of adaptations, in other words an education in oblivion.' (*Discusión*, pp. 69, 70)

In an essay on H. G. Wells he writes: 'When he (Wells) descends to the level of pure reason, we know he is fallible. Reality is inferred from events, not reasonings.' (*Inquisitions*, p. 88) and in the prologue to *Historia de la Eternidad* he admits: 'I place no faith in interpretations, not even in mine.'

Alicia Jurado maintains in this connection:

'We must never forget that his intelligence, which is always alert, is at the service of games rather than convictions.... The purpose of the game is not to discover incognizable reality; it has an aesthetic aim.' (*Genio*, p. 60)

'All of Borges' works – poems, essays and especially tales – express this game against an unknown opponent that he is unwilling to name, through intellectual honesty.' (*Genio*, p. 66) However, 'There is one thing of which he could never be accused, and that is frivolity; the game is never insignificant nor is the bet trivial.... Borges plays, but this is a dangerous game in which his destiny, which at the same time is ours, is at stake.' (*Genio*, p. 67)

In the prologue to his *Obra Poetica*, Borges himself deals with this error when he states that although in his opinion the aesthetic factor is the main one, this is far from being solely an entertaining game.

'What is essential is the aesthetic factor, the thrill, the physical effect brought about by reading.... Literature imposes its magic by means of artifices; the reader finally recognizes them and scorns them; this is why there is a constant need for minor or substantial variations, that can bring back the past or foreshadow the future.'

Borges' game is thus seen to be a technique that he uses to

convey a really effective message to each reader, one that is capable of transforming him and helping him to understand his own destiny and the complex reality that surrounds him.

'Work that endures is always capable of an infinite and plastic ambiguity; it is all things to all men, like the Apostle; it is a mirror that reflects the reader's own traits and it is also a map of the world.' (*Inquisitions*, p. 87)

Borges does not think that the ordinary literal language can achieve this objective and this is why he resorts to artifice.

'It is hazardous to think that a co-ordination of words (philosophies are nothing else) can have much resemblance to the Universe.' (*Inquisitions*, p. 114)

Ana María Barrenechea says:

'He has strong misgivings about this instrument, the purpose of which he humorously attributes to the Devil: "Language is like the moon, it has its hemisphere of darkness"....

'As a writer Borges feels that experiences are ineffable, because it is useless to try to express, with words that everyone can understand, the uniqueness of each individual and each circumstance....

'He thinks that as human beings we are obliged to communicate by means of words and that we are obliged also to use metaphors and allegories, that is to say deceit.' (*Labyrinth*, pp. 79, 80)

In this connection, Borges writes:

'Allegories, for example, offer the reader a double or triple intuition, not a handful of characters who can be replaced by abstract nouns.... From this I venture to infer that it is absurd to reduce a story to its moral, a parable merely to its purpose, a "form" to its "content".' (*Discusión*, pp. 163, 164)

'The frantic desire to reach a conclusion is the most disastrous and sterile of manias. Art necessarily works through symbols.' (*Discusión*, p. 141)

This means that Borges is not interested in the literal truth of words but in the effect they produce.

Ana María Barrenechea refers to this trait in the following terms:

'Harassed by an excessively real but at the same time meaningless world, he tries to free himself of his obsession by creating another phantasmagoric world which is so coherent that it creates doubts in our minds, a world which is the denial of the very same reality that we had been relying on.

'To undermine our belief in a concrete existence, Borges attacks the basic principles on which the safety of life itself is founded: the universe, personality and time.' (*Labyrinth*, p. 16)

Alicia Jurado further points out:

'In an essay, "The Dream of Coleridge" (*Inquisitions*, p. 14), after imagining different interpretations, his true inclination is revealed in a sentence that gives him away: "The hypotheses that transcend reason are much more appealing." ' (*Genio*, p. 61)

Borges leads us to suspect that reality moves in dimensions that transcend reason and that our perceptions are mere dreams:

'We (the undivided divinity that operates within us) have dreamed the world. We have dreamed it strong, mysterious, visible, ubiquitous in space and secure in time; but we have allowed tenuous eternal interstices of injustice in its structure so that we may know that it is false.' (*Inquisitions*, p. 115)

However, the intention of this irrationality in Borges' works is not to destroy us nor to condemn us to 'a frozen and futureless destiny', as Adolfo Prieto maintains. In her conclusion, Ana María Barrenechea explains:

'However, let us not arrive at a false and negative conclusion concerning Borges' work. . . . This nihilistic concept could be demolished simply by means of some of the observations that we have made. . . . The most powerful one perhaps is the creative pleasure of the author, who sees in other imaginations and in his own the real force that is capable of transcending the limitations of our human condition.' (*Labyrinth*, p. 145) This means that he does not destroy our beliefs and then abandon us; he does it so as to give us, through his works, sufficient strength for us to transcend the limitations of our ordinary approach.

In the ideal world that Borges postulates in 'Tlön, Uqbar, Orbis Tertius' (*Fictions*, p. 17), he says:

'The books themselves are also odd. Works of fiction are based on a single plot, which runs through every imaginable permutation. Works of natural philosophy invariably include thesis and antithesis, the strict pro and con of a theory. A book which does not include its opposite, or "counterbook", is considered incomplete.' (p. 28)

In his essay, 'Two Books' (*Inquisitions*, p. 129), he mentions the fact that Bertrand Russell proposes that primary schools should teach children to read the newspapers with incredulity. ' "That Socratic discipline would be useful, I believe".' He proposes such work as this:

' "A typical assignment would be to read about the history of the wars with France in English textbooks, and then to rewrite that history from the French viewpoint." ' (p. 131)

The procedures that Borges postulates are so similar to the ones he applies, when developing simultaneously different parallel and even contrary theories on a single subject, that they reveal 'his own game' as a technique that also has a definite aim. Borges tries to free us from thinking in patterns and to increase the range of our thoughts, leading them along new paths. Borges is not ignorant of nor does he reject the possibility of a fuller development for the human mind, a development which would enable man to perceive different characteristics and dimensions of reality.

Writing about Gerald Heard (*Discusión*, p. 166), he says that Heard asserts the possibility of a rapid evolution of the human faculties and mentions previous writers who have postulated similar theories. He says: 'Like Edward Carpenter, like Leadbetter, like Dunne, Ouspensky prophesies that our minds will dispense with linear and successive time and will know the universe intuitively, in an angelic way, *sub specie aeternitatis*.' (p. 169) Borges concludes with his personal opinion: 'That the perception of truth will somehow evolve does not seem unlikely to me, and it is probably inevitable; that it will be a very abrupt evolution seems to me to be a gratuitous assertion by the author, an artificial stimulant.' (p. 169)

In her book, Ana María Barrenechea lays emphasis on this angelic possession of the universe; it consists of direct, intuitive or mystical perception of truth, a principle acknowledged by Borges throughout his works. (*Labyrinth*, pp. 82–85) Of Pascal, Borges says:

'He is not a mystic; he belongs to those Christians, denounced by Swedenborg, who suppose that heaven is a reward and hell a punishment and who, accustomed to melancholy meditation, do not know how to speak with the angels.' (*Inquisitions*, p. 95)

Borges frequently uses religious terms, though with a meaning which differs from the ordinary one, since he knows about 'their guilty condition of being mere metaphors.' (*Discusión*, p. 57) He is an enthusiastic investigator of all the Holy Scriptures because of the various meanings hidden behind the outward context. 'Origenes attributed three meanings to the words of the Scriptures: the historical, the moral and the mystical. ... Erigena, an infinite number of meanings, like the iridescent colours of the peacock's plumage.' (*Discusión*, p. 59 *fn.*)

In 'Una Vindicación de la Cábala' (*Discusión*, p. 55), he says:

'I do not want to vindicate the doctrine but the hermeneutic or cryptographic procedures that lead to it. These procedures, as is well-known, are the vertical reading of sacred texts, the method of reading called *boustrophedon* (reading one line from right to left and the next from left to right), methodically substituting certain letters of the alphabet for others, adding up the numerical value of the letters, etc. It is easy to scoff at these operations, I would rather try to understand them.' (p. 55)

In the Epilogue to *Other Inquisitions, 1937–1952* he says:

'As I corrected the proofs of this volume, I discovered two tendencies in these miscellaneous essays. The first tendency is to evaluate religious or philosophical ideas on the basis of their aesthetic worth and even for what is singular and marvellous about them. Perhaps this is an indication of a basic scepticism. The other tendency is to presuppose (and to verify) that the number of fables and metaphors of which men's imagination is capable is limited, but that these few inventions can be all things to all men, like the Apostle.' (*Inquisitions*, p. 189)

As regards his religious views, in an appendix to *Discusión* Borges writes:

'I have venerated the gradual invention of God; Hell and Heaven (eternal reward, eternal punishment) are alike admirable and curious products of man's imagination.

'Theologians define Heaven as a place of everlasting glory and happiness and advise us that this is not the place devoted to

infernal torments. The fourth chapter of this book[1] very reasonably
denies this division, arguing that Hell and Heaven are not topo-
graphical locations, but extreme states of the soul. . . . Weatherhead
is a mediocre and as it were non-existent writer, stimulated by
pious readings, yet he knows intuitively that the direct pursuit of
unalloyed and perpetual happiness will be no less ridiculous on
the other side of death than it is on this. He writes: "The
highest conception of the joyous experiences that we have called
Heaven is that of service: it is that of full and free participation
in the work of Christ. This could happen among other spirits,
perhaps in other worlds; maybe we can help in saving our own . . .
the more we have evolved in this world, the more we shall be able
to share in God's life in the next." . . .

'I do not know what the reader will think of such semi-
theosophical conjectures[2]. Catholics (that is to say Argentine
Catholics) believe in a world beyond this one, but I have noticed
that they do not take any interest in it. With me it is the reverse; I
am interested but I do not believe in it.' (*Discusión*, pp. 172–174)

There is a most significant postscript to Borges' essay, 'La
Duración del Infierno' (*Discusión*, p. 97):

'On this page, which contains simply information, I may perhaps
also report a dream. I dreamed that I was awaking from another
dream – full of cataclysms and turmoil – and that I was waking up
in a room which I did not recognize. Dawn was breaking: a
faint, diffused light outlined the foot of the iron bedstead, the
narrow chair, the door and the window, both closed, the white
table. I thought fearfully "Where am I?" and realized that I did
not know. I thought "Who am I?" and I could not recognize
myself. Fear grew within me. I thought: "This distressing awakening is already Hell, this awakening without a future will be my
eternity." Then I really awoke, trembling.' (p. 102)

Not to know oneself, not to know one's destiny, that is the real
hell for Borges.

Alicia Jurado writes:

'Borges views the dogmas of all religions from the same sceptical
standpoint, and instead of considering them truths that have been

[1] Leslie D. Weatherhead: *After Death* (London, 1942).
[2] 'Theosophy used Sufism', see *Way*, p. 15.

revealed and are unquestionable, he sees in them only different ways of interpreting, within the limitations of human experience, a spiritual truth that is beyond the reach of reason. . . .

'However, God appears frequently in Borges' writings, though in an abstract manner and devoid of theological attributes. . . .

'His poems and tales frequently refer to experiences of a mystical nature. "The Zahir" and "The Aleph" are well-known. In the first tale there is a twenty-cent coin that obsesses anyone who might possess it, and the main character in the story, already on the verge of madness, reflects: "The Sufis, attempting to lose themselves in God, repeat their own name or the ninety-nine names of the Divinity until they lose all meaning. Perhaps I shall manage to wear away the Zahir by dint of thinking of it and thinking of it. Perhaps behind the Zahir I shall find God." The "aleph" is a dot in space that contains the universe; it corresponds therefore to the contemplation of the Divinity. . . .

'Nearer yet to the authentic mystical experience is that which overtakes the Aztec priest Tzinacán in the story 'La Escritura del Dios'. He saw "infinite processes that made up a single happiness" and he was filled with the sensation of understanding it all, which is so characteristic of mystical rapture and which St. John tried to describe in an explanatory chapter of the 'Spiritual Canticle'. . . .

'Other writings mention the states of the soul that resemble a faint, confused intuition of God. One reads in "The End": "There is an hour of the afternoon when the plain is on the verge of saying something; it never says it or perhaps it says it infinitely, or perhaps we do not understand it, or we understand it but it is as untranslatable as music." This is simply a presentiment of incomplete revelations. In other pages that are often quoted, "Sentirse en muerte", Borges refers to an experience of his which he uses to "refute" time. Wandering through out-of-the-way corners of the city, he comes across a poor street with a pink wall and a fig tree showing above it, and this modest scene transports him to another place, not through imagination but by direct intuition of eternity: "I felt I was dead – that I was an abstract perceiver of the world; I felt an undefined fear imbued with knowledge, the supreme clarity of metaphysics. No, I did not believe I had sailed up the so-called waters of Time; rather I suspected I was the possessor of the elusive or non-existent meaning of the inconceivable word *eternity*." (*Inquisitions*, p. 180)

'Few people have noticed Borges' connections with mysticism; one of them was Estela Canto. In a review of the tales in *El Aleph*, which she called narratives, essays and also legends, she said: "The universe, its apparent contradictions, its hidden meanings and man's anxiety on being faced with it are clearly depicted in all of Borges' tales. One of the characteristics of mystical thinkers is that they are inclined to express themselves by means of symbols. I would say that the best definition of Borges is that he is one of the greatest – and they are extremely rare – mystical thinkers of our time." *Mystical thinker*, naturally, not just *mystic*.' (*Genio*, pp. 76–80)

I agree with her that Borges is a mystical thinker rather than a mystic. I see in these stories a technique for stimulating thought rather than conveying literal meanings. Once we have lost our faith in reason as a means of seeking truth, Borges does not abandon us but opens up a new range of possibilities by following the path of intuition. By repeatedly bringing us face to face with perceptions of such extraordinary reach, in stories in which he himself often plays the part of the hero, Borges' intention is to bring us near to this type of experience, as well as to the minor intuitions that abound in his writings, for example to the knowledge of our real destiny, which is generally revealed in a direct way and where reason would least have expected it. Borges is trying in this way to familiarize us with intuition, a kind of knowledge that man no longer takes into account and which he has completely forgotten. Much criticism of the destructiveness of the author's writings is based on the fact that he plunges his characters into a world of chaos and chance, but this happens only when they search obsessively for the meaning of life through their own reasoning or in books.

Alicia Jurado maintains that destiny appears as the reverse of chance in Borges' work (*Genio*, p. 84). Certainty and confidence are attained by fulfilling one's own destiny. Various characters in Borges' stories manage to discover their destiny, but it is always through an intuitive and direct vision, an instantaneous comprehension, not a rational elaboration.

'He realized (beyond words and even beyond understanding) that he could not cope with the city. . . .

'Any life, no matter how long or complex it may be, is made up essentially *of a single moment* – the moment in which a man finds out, once and for all, who he is. . . . To Tadeo Isidoro Cruz, who did not know how to read, this revelation was not given by a book.' (*Aleph*, pp. 82, 83)

In the 'Story of the Warrior and the Captive', the barbarian who goes over to the cause of Rome and is 'suddenly blinded and renewed by the sight of the City' . . . 'was not a traitor (traitors do not inspire pious epitaphs), he was a visionary, a convert.'

And again:

'The figure of the barbarian who embraces the cause of Ravenna and the figure of the European woman who chooses the wilderness may seem antithetical. Nevertheless, both were carried away by a secret impulse, an impulse deeper than reason, and both obeyed this impulse they could not have justified.' (*Anthology*, pp. 172, 174)

The librarian in 'The Secret Miracle', tells how he and his ancestors had all gone blind in a useless search for God in the letters of the vast number of volumes the library contains.

'A reader came in to return an atlas. "This atlas is useless", he said, and handed it to Hladik, who opened it at random. As if through a haze, he saw a map of India. With a sudden rush of assurance, he touched one of the tiniest letters. A ubiquitous voice said: "The time for your work has been granted".' (*Fictions*, p. 134)

The main character in 'La Escritura del Dios' wakes up from his nightmare and suddenly discovers, on looking up and seeing a light, that instead of being a priest of the god or an avenger, he is a prisoner. (*El Aleph*, p. 122)

In 'The Approach to Al-Mu'tasim', the principal character 'arrives at a mysterious conviction: some place in the world there is a man from whom this clarity emanates; some place in the world there is a man who is this clarity. The student resolves to dedicate his life to finding him.' (*Fictions*, p. 38)

Through this knowledge of their own destiny, the situation of the characters changes immediately in our eyes, from the uncertain and helpless initial state to one of certainty, in which they are confident and at peace with themselves, a state which even becomes joy. Laprida says, in 'Conjectural Poem':

> 'I who longed to be someone else, to weigh
> judgments, to read books, to hand down the law,
> will lie in the open out in these swamps;
> but a secret joy somehow swells my breast.
> I see at last that I am face to face
> with my South American destiny.
> I was carried to this ruinous hour
> by the intricate labyrinth of steps
> woven by my days from a day that goes
> back to my birth. At last I've discovered
> the mysterious key to all my years'   (*Anthology*, p. 192)

Dahlmann, the hero of the tale 'The South',
'As he crossed the threshold ... felt that to die in a knife fight, under the open sky, and going forward to the attack, would have been a liberation, a joy, and a festive occasion. On the first night in the sanatorium, when they stuck the needle in him, he felt that if he had been able to choose then, or to dream his death, this would have been the death he would have chosen or dreamt.' (*Fictions*, p. 159)

In the 'Story of the Warrior and the Captive',
'An Englishwoman had lowered herself to this barbarism. Shocked and pitiful, my grandmother urged her not to return and promised to protect her and to rescue her children. The woman answered that she was happy, and that night returned to the wilderness.' (*Anthology*, p. 173)

The real destiny that Borges alludes to is in every case a collective one.

'It was as if the South had resolved that Dahlmann should accept the duel.' (*Fictions*, p. 158)

'Yes, but Damián, as a gaucho, should have been Martín Fierro. ... If destiny brings me another battle, I'll be ready for it.

For forty years he waited and waited, with an inarticulate hope, and then in the end, at the hour of his death, fate brought him his battle.' (*Aleph*, pp. 106, 109)

In 'The Garden of Forking Paths', the spy says:

'I carried out my plan because I felt the Chief had some fear of those of my race, of those uncountable forebears whose culmination lies in me. I wished to prove to him that a yellow man could save his armies.' (*Fictions*, p. 83)

And the German in 'Deutsches Requiem' says:

'I realized, however, that we were on the verge of a new era which, like the initial period of Islam or Christianity, required a new man.' (*El Aleph*, p. 85)

In order to take part in this collective destiny, the characters have to give up a merely individual destiny, which apparently offers them more possibilities and advantages. They have to transcend their immediate circumstances and experience their interrelation with the complex organism of life that surrounds them. Cruz foregoes the advantages of keeping within the law; Laprida abandons his initial longing to weigh judgments and read books in order to take part in the South American destiny, which implies the success of the 'montoneros' (group of revolutionary horsemen); the captive woman renounces civilization; the warrior knows that in the City 'he will be a dog, or a child, and that he will not even begin to understand it, but that it is worth more than all his gods'. (*Anthology*, p. 171)

In order to fulfil his destiny, the Nazi, in 'Deutsches Requiem', had to eliminate his mercifulness:

'My years of training were harder for me than for many of the others, because, although I was not lacking in courage, I had no inclination towards violence.... I hated my comrades individually. ... Many things have to be destroyed to build a new system; now we know that Germany was one of them.' (*El Aleph*, pp. 85, 86, 91)

The Aztec priest in 'La Escritura del Dios' foregoes the power that he has obtained through his knowledge of the divine formula:

'I need only say it to get out of this prison of stone, for day to enter my night, in order to be young, to be immortal, for the tiger to destroy Alvarado, to plunge the holy knife into Spanish chests,

to rebuild the pyramid, to rebuild the empire.' (*El Aleph*, p. 123)
In order to pursue the real universal destiny, he foregoes not
only his individual destiny but also that of his whole nation and
abandons the possibility of vindicating his people.

'Whoever has glimpsed the universe, whoever has glimpsed the
ardent purposes of the universe, cannot think of one man and of
his trivial moments of happiness or misfortune, even though that
man be himself. That man *has been himself* and now he does not
care. What does he care about that man's fate, about that man's
nation, if he is now nobody? This is why I will not recite the
formula, this is why I will lie in darkness and let the days forget
me.' (*El Aleph*, p. 123)

What is remarkable in all the characters who follow their
destiny is the real detachment from their own interests with which
they face the fulfilling of their real role on earth. Tadeo Isidoro
Cruz 'understood that one destiny is no better than another, but
that every man must obey what is within him' and he acted
accordingly, without thinking about the dangers and difficulties
with which he would now be faced. In 'La Casa de Asterión',
from the moment the Minotaur knew that one day his redeemer
would come, he happily awaited his destiny, which was death.
'Would you believe it, Ariadne?' said Theseus, 'the Minotaur
barely defended himself.' (*El Aleph*, p. 72)

The Nazi concludes:

'If victory, injustice and happiness are not for Germany, then let
them be for other nations. I look at my face in the mirror to see
who I am and to see how I will behave in a few hours, when I
face my end. My flesh may be afraid, but not I.' (*El Aleph*, p. 92)

Almost at the end of 'The South':

'They went out and if Dahlmann was without hope, he was
also without fear. . . . Firmly clutching his knife, which he perhaps
would not know how to wield, Dahlmann went out into the plain.'
(*Fictions*, p. 159)

In 'Three Versions of Judas',

'The treachery of Judas was not accidental; it was a predestined
deed which has its mysterious place in the economy of the Re-
demption. . . . Judas, alone among the apostles, intuited the secret
divinity and the terrible purpose of Jesus. The Word had lowered

Himself to be mortal; Judas, the disciple of the Word, could lower himself to the role of informer (the worst transgression dishonour abides) and welcome the fire which can not be extinguished. . . . He renounced honour, good, peace, the Kingdom of Heaven, as others, less heroically, renounced pleasure.' (*Fictions*, pp. 139, 140)

In 'Theme of the Traitor and Hero', Kilpatrick

'signed his own death sentence; but he implored that his condemnation should not be allowed to hurt the fatherland. . . . (He) swore to collaborate in a project which allowed him the opportunity to redeem himself and which would add a flourish to his death. . . . carried away by the minutely scrupulous destiny which redeemed and condemned him, (he) more than once enriched (Nolan's) text with words and deeds of his own improvization.' (*Fictions*, pp. 114, 115)

Hladik, in 'The Secret Miracle', finally rids himself of his fear and, accepting his execution, does not ask for the miracle of his own salvation but to be able to fulfil his destiny.

'He had asked God for an entire year in which to finish his work: His omnipotence had granted him the time. For his sake, God projected a secret miracle. . . . He did not work for posterity, nor even for God, of whose literary preferences he possessed scant knowledge. Meticulous, unmoving, secretive, he wove his lofty, invisible labyrinth in time. He worked the third act over twice. He eliminated some rather too-obvious symbols.' (*Fictions*, p. 136)

To enable his characters to fulfil their destiny, Borges rids them of all preconceived rigid morals. Alicia Jurado points out that 'the idea of guilt is non-existent in Borges. In fact we do not find a single ethical judgment, whether explicit or implicit, in his works; like the hypothetical God, for whom the victim and the aggressor form a single person, Borges does not sympathize with any of his characters nor does he worry about the problem of good and bad. (One must not infer that the same thing happens in the citizen Borges, who is most definite in his moral views.)' (*Genio*, p. 105)

When Alicia Jurado says that Borges does not sympathize with any of his characters and that the personal opinions of the citizen do not influence the author, she is pinpointing one of the characteristics of his writing which has perhaps most contributed to the confusion and the misguided views of Borges' work. Borges makes his characters accord with the circumstances which surround them in each case and not with his subjective point of view. All the different races, nationalities and periods, with their widely varying trends, are depicted in his works. He is probably one of the most objective authors to have covered such a wide and complex panorama of humanity.

There is no point in searching through Borges' work for personal trends that might define his particular philosophical, religious or political doctrine. Many of those who criticize his 'apparent' political views would be surprised to discover that the author gives a certain human backing to all his characters on an equal basis, without sympathizing with any of their principles, whether they are English, Nazis, Jews, Arabs or Asian. Many of our nationalists, who accuse him of being a Liberal, would be amazed at his earnest attempts, described in 'Deutsches Requiem', to understand the destiny which our Germanophiles – who know nothing of Germany, as Borges himself states in the postscript to *El Aleph* – are incapable of recognizing or even suspecting. In this story he has written what probably constitutes the best defence that can be made of the head of a Nazi extermination camp. They would also be surprised to learn that, far from suggesting that the Argentines should follow the path dreamed of by Laprida and the men of books and theories, Borges recommends the opposite. The South American destiny is represented by the South, by the courage of the 'montoneros', by the interior of the country, as Borges confirms in his 'Conjectural Poem' and in his tales 'The South', 'The Life of Tadeo Isidoro Cruz', 'The End', 'The Story of the Warrior and the Captive', 'The Other Death', etc. They would be surprised to discover a certain admiration for those characters of his who resolutely take up the knife, or for the English girl who renounces civilization to pursue the primitive South American destiny, perhaps as 'a challenge or a symbol'.

Alicia Jurado asserts that if there is one tendency the author does display in his books, it is admiration for physical courage.

'The only characteristics described as despicable are cowardice and betrayal: in short, primitive ethics, much more typical of primitive people than of the complex European cultures whose influence on Borges some deplore.' (*Genio*, p. 105)

Borges' essay, 'Two Books', clarifies things for us. He first comments on a book written by H. G. Wells (*Guide to the New World*) and 'the doctrine contained in this revolutionary manual, which can be summarized in this precise dilemma: either Britain identifies her cause with that of a general revolution (with that of a federated world), or victory is inaccessible and vain. Chapter XII establishes the basic principles of the new world.... Wells admonishes us to remember our essential humanity and to suppress our miserable differential traits, no matter how pathetic or picturesque they may be.... We are urged to reconsider the history of the world without geographical, economic or ethnic preferences.' (*Inquisitions*, p. 130–131) After this comes the comment, mentioned earlier, on a book written by Bertrand Russell, who also advises universalism and proposes the task for the school-child of rewriting the history of the wars with France from the French point of view, after having studied them in English text-books.

Borges leads us to suspect, in his own way, that is in a disguised manner and by reading between the lines, that this is precisely his real inclination. He admits that for him there are no differences between men: 'the inevitable and *trivial* circumstance of having been born in a certain country and of belonging to a certain race.... I generally find the difference between Jews and non-Jews quite insignificant, and sometimes illusory or imperceptible.... I quoted the wise declaration of Mark Twain: "I do not ask what race a man belongs to; it is enough for me to know that he is a human being, nobody can be anything worse".' (*Inquisitions*, p. 130–131)

This explains why Borges shows no preference for any of his characters and why he tries to justify them all, equally, as human beings. He is trying to convey a message of brotherhood and togetherness among mankind. He points out the limitations of all theories and doctrines with the object of tearing down false frontiers that divide men. And when he lays emphasis on courage and loyalty, which are primitive virtues, he does so precisely because of their primitiveness, which makes them common to all humanity.

Guide-lines of Borges' Thought

To summarize the main lines of Borges' ideas, then, the following points can be made:

For Borges, the main objective of art is to help the reader to accomplish his own art, which is to know his own self and the world, in other words to know his real role in the economy of the world. Borges emphasizes the need to identify oneself with the collective destiny and to give up the merely individual one.

A work of art is of no use in transmitting doctrines nor in trying to explain reality theoretically. Words, which are mere abstract concepts, cannot cover all the complex circumstances that surround each particular person.

Knowledge of one's own destiny requires a direct vision of it and a constant study of the possibilities. But our perceptions are selective and deformed because of our subjective approach and our attempts to rationalize these perceptions.

Therefore to help the reader to discover reality and to leave his individualism behind, Borges seeks to develop his capacity for understanding by means of all kinds of mental exercises. Borges' writings are designed to produce certain impacts on the reader. By bringing him face to face with transcendental problems he tries to confuse him, to get him out of thinking in rigid patterns, to destroy his primitive beliefs, to make him doubt his own mental powers and to face him constantly with a world full of irrational elements and aspects of reality that can be known intuitively but which cannot be explained. He tries to destroy his faith in his reasoning and make him admit the possibility of a reality that cannot be rationally explained.

He accustoms the reader to wider and more objective approaches by simultaneously developing all the possible interpretations of one aspect of reality, or else by showing him the least known sides of reality.

And to achieve the *thrill*, the aesthetic factor, the physical transformation produced by reading, in other words to produce the desired effect on the reader, Borges resorts to literary artifice. He uses the language of symbols, which is ambiguous and has multiple and hidden meanings, some of which are only hinted at, and renounces literal and verbal language in favour of a more suggestive and expressive one, more suited to intuition than to rational understanding.

In the next chapter I shall deal with the coincidences between the guide-lines of Borges' thought and the principles of the Sufis, as they appear in the themes chosen and the techniques employed.

IV
Thematic Coincidences

○☞

The Infinite

The theme of the infinite underlies all Sufi literature, as it does Borges' writings. The most varied topics imply something that is beyond which has immeasurable and infinite dimensions. 'The infinite universe lies beyond this world' is a thought expressed by the poet Rumi, on which the Sufis suggest we meditate. This meditation can be found in Borges' writings, where it becomes a metaphysical search, underlying all the philosophical and theological hypotheses contained in his works.

Ana María Barrenechea lays special emphasis on this subject:

'Borges knows that all reality melts away in the presence of the infinite and he continually summons the infinite in his works. He sometimes refers to it in one word and at other times develops a complex argument on it. . . .

'The projection of blurred horizons and unattainable objectives contributes to the dream-like and anxiety-filled atmosphere that envelopes his tales. In "Averroës' Search" (*Anthology*, p. 101), Borges has expressed the oppressive feeling that this idea of vastness produces when simply mentioned: "The fear of gross infinitude, of mere space, of matter alone struck Averroës for a moment. He looked at the symmetrical garden; he realized that he was old, useless and unreal." ' (*Labyrinth*, p. 24)

In the Sufi tale, 'Paradise of Song', when Ahangar returns from his search in the Valley of Paradise:

'He looked at the assembled people with a weariness and hopelessness that he had never felt before. He said: "I climbed and I climbed, and I climbed. When it seemed as though there could be no human habitation in such a desolate place, and after many trials and disappointments, I came upon a valley." . . . Ahangar rapidly grew old and died. And all the people, every one who had heard this story from the lips of Ahangar, first lost heart in their lives, then grew old and died, for they felt that something was going to happen over which they had no control and from which they had no hope, and so they lost interest in life itself.

It is only once in a thousand years that this secret is seen by man.' (*Wisdom*, pp. 79, 80)

To quote Ana María Barrenechea again:

'Borges refers to the infinite through great time cycles; we notice that he projects the tale back to a very remote past, the manifestation of which becomes gradually more intense and finally places it beyond time, in eternity. . . .

'The characters are also encompassed within large geographical boundaries. . . . India, especially, is useful to him as a metaphor of the universe, with the double reference to its vastness and its chaotic situation.' (*Labyrinth*, p. 29)

Hladik, in 'The Secret Miracle', finds God and also His almighty key, and India is an adequate setting for the unending postponements of 'The Approach to Al-Mu'tasim'. (*Fictions*, pp. 130, 135)

The Sufi tales in general go back to the distant past and take place in vast settings. In 'Fatima the Spinner and the Tent', Fatima, from the Farthest West, is shipwrecked once again and is cast up on the seashore of a strange land and from there reaches China, which was her destiny. In the tales 'Maruf the Cobbler', 'The Man whose Time was Wrong', 'The Four Magic Treasures', 'The Merchant and the Christian Dervish', 'The Story of Tea', etc., long journeys are made from one end of the world to the other. (*Dervishes*, pp. 72, 162, 158, 108, 46, 88)

Ana María Barrenechea points out that often the idea of infinitude is more forcefully expressed by simultaneously uniting spatial and temporal vastness:

'Then distant times and places aim at this miraculous union and will fulfil their mystery through the projection of infinitude.

'The symmetry of Kubla Khan's dreams, that take in continents and centuries, is magically achieved in both areas, but especially in the temporal dimension, to prepare the way for revelation. In 'The Enigma of Edward Fitzgerald', he points out the distance between both the countries and the periods of time that separate Omar Khayyam, the Persian poet, from his English translator and diffuser.' (*Inquisitions*, pp. 14, 75; *Labyrinth*, p. 32)

Often the characters or elements that are not hindered by human limitations of time or space achieve the effect of the infinite. This is the case of the narrator of 'The Immortal' (*El Aleph*, p. 7) who ends the story remembering his last thousand years of life spent in different places in the world, and of Khidr, the immortal guide of the Sufis, who appears and, after transmitting his message, disappears. Or of the characters of the tales that are common to both literatures: the genie imprisoned in the bottle or the Angel of Death.

But it is in mystical experiences that the vastness of time and space gains greater dimensions and the reader is faced with the infinite universe, through a direct and complete vision of the extremely complex reality.

'The shattering and pathetic effect produced by the presence of this double infinity of time and space is accentuated by the narrating of facts or by the superposition of images in concentric circles that gradually increase in size and become included the one in the other....

'The very structure of the tales can evoke multiplicity through reflections and bifurcations, complicated at times by cyclic repetition....

'A tale with a Chinese box structure: unreal worlds lying one within the other and at the same time within this world which disintegrates on contact with such phantasmagorias....

'His work abounds in these series of links in linear or cyclic form that always suggest the infinite.... He recalls Kafka and the Zohar, with its unending series of portals which lead to Glory. In the case of 'The Arabian Nights', he emphasizes its eternal circle. He is much interested in dilemma syllogisms, which are also a cyclic type of reasoning and he increases the stock of them with an example of his own.' (*Labyrinth*, pp. 33, 37, 38, 45)

The syllogisms to which Ana María Barrenechea refers and which Borges calls 'dilemma syllogisms' are of the following type:

'Democritus swears that the Abderitans are liars; but Democritus is an Abderitan; therefore Democritus lies; therefore it is not true that the Abderitans are liars; therefore Democritus lies; therefore it is not true that the Abderitans are liars; therefore Democritus lies. . . . There are almost innumerable versions depending on the same method, though the characters and the fables vary. . . . To these illustrious perplexities I venture to add this one: There is a person in Sumatra who wants to become a fortune-teller. The magician-examiner asks him whether he thinks he will fail or pass the test. The candidate replies that he will fail. The unending sequel can be foreseen.' (*Discusión*, p. 166)

These very same characteristics, which Ana María Barrenechea links with the infinite, are to be found in Sufi literature. Many stories are set in the distant past but continue the narrative through stories within the story that have taken place long before, just as in the traditional tales of 'The Arabian Nights', which Borges often quotes and which the Sufis consider to be teaching stories in their original version.

The theme of waiting at a door[1] appears in 'The Gates of Paradise' (*Dervishes*, p. 75) but the similarity with Borges' work is perhaps greater when reference is made to the many barriers that separate the seeker from his goal in tales like 'The Food of Paradise' (*Dervishes*, p. 15) and 'Paradise of Song' (*Wisdom*, p. 77).

Examples of dilemma syllogisms are plentiful in Sufi writings, for instance: 'Truth is something which I never speak' (*Sufis*, p. 97), meaning, among other things, 'If this is true, he is lying; if it is not true, he is telling the truth', and so on.

And again:

'A voice whispered to me last night: "There is no such thing as a voice whispering in the night!"' (*Wisdom*, p. 146)

The useless and untiring attempts to reach a goal whose attainment sends the seeker back to the starting point is a theme frequently encountered in both literatures. In 'The Library of Babel', the endless postponements that appear to be one of the answers to the search are finally replaced by another of a cyclic nature, which the author presents in this way: 'The library is limitless and periodic. If an eternal voyager were to traverse it in any direction, he would find, after many centuries, that the same

---

[1] This is a symbol that has strong links with Sufism since *dervish* is derived from the Persian verb *der vekhtan*, which means to wait at a door, the reference being to waiting at the door of enlightenment.

volumes are repeated in the same disorder (which repeated, would constitute an order: Order itself). (*Fictions*, p. 80)

Ana María Barrenechea writes:

'The Approach to Al-Mu'tasim' (*Fictions*, p. 35) tells of the search for a man through the reflections he has left in other men, in the guise of a tale of the complex and chaotic adventures that take place during a cyclic pilgrimage through Hindustan. But the search itself suggests the possibility of never reaching the goal, illustrated by the two diagrams of the infinite straight line and the circle.... The fact that the novel begins and ends in the same place in Bombay is again an allusion to the eternal return, the theme with which Borges links the postponements and regressions in his works.' (*Labyrinth*, p. 44)

This is how the story of 'Averroës' Search' (*Anthology*, p. 101) half finishes, turned ironically upon itself:

'I sensed that Averroës, striving to imagine a drama without ever having suspected what a theatre is, was no more absurd than I, who strove to imagine Averroës with no material other than some fragments from Renan, Lane and Asín Palacios. I sensed, on the last page, that my narrative was a symbol of the man I was while I wrote it, and that to write that story I had to be that man and to be that man, I had to write that story, and so on to infinity.' (p. 110)

Borges has written two essays and a poem, 'The Cyclical Night' (*Anthology*, p. 155), on the doctrine of the eternal return and he refers fleetingly to cyclic time in 'Theme of the Traitor and Hero', 'The Garden of Forking Paths', 'Three Versions of Judas', 'Tlön, Uqbar, Orbis Tertius', 'The Library of Babel' (*Fictions*, pp. 112, 81, 138, 17, 72) and 'The Immortal' (*El Aleph*, p. 7).

This circular movement is also a characteristic of Sufi literature. In 'The Food of Paradise' (*Dervishes*, p. 15), after many adventures the seeker discovers the truth, which takes him back to the starting point and indicates an unending linking of relative values, since what for him is the food of paradise is merely a residue for a princess. In 'The Fruit of Heaven' and 'Ahrar and the Wealthy Couple' (*Wisdom*, pp. 11, 19), after a long pilgrimage and quest, the seekers end their search by returning to one of the teachers that they had rejected at the beginning of their journey.

There are many allegories of man's destiny in which man is depicted as estranged from and oblivious of his origins, to which he must finally return. For example, in the tale of 'The Islanders' (*Sufis*, p. 1), the people had to learn to swim in order to be able to return to their original home.

In 'The Woman Sufi and the Queen' (*Wisdom*, p. 111), the course of history repeats itself in the attitude of the Queen, who has the same characteristics as her hated predecessors. In 'The Tale of the Sands' (*Dervishes*, p. 23), the allegory refers to cyclic time and the eternal return, expressed in the destiny of the stream (life) which the wind takes up and carries as vapour and then lets fall again as rain so that it becomes a river again, a process that continues for ever.

' "We know because we see it happen every day, and because we, the sands, extend from the riverside all the way to the mountain." '

'And that is why it is said that the way in which the Stream of Life is to continue on its journey is written in the Sands.' (p. 24)

The tale 'Paradise of Song' (*Wisdom*, p. 77) illustrates another of the theories to which Borges frequently refers. Ahangar returns from his journey to the Valley of Paradise and says:

' "This valley was exactly like the one in which we live. And then I saw the people: they are *the same people*. For every Hasan, every Aisha, every Ahangar, every anybody whom we have here, there is another one, exactly the same, in that valley.

"These are likenesses and reflections to us, when we see such things. But it is we who are the likeness and reflection of them – we who are here, we are their twins . . .".' (p. 80)

Borges says in 'Three Versions of Judas' (*Fictions*, p. 138):

'The lower sphere is a reflection of the higher sphere; the shapes on earth correspond to those in Heaven; the marks on the skin are a map of the incorruptible stars.' (p. 140)

In his essay 'The Mirror of the Enigmas' (*Inquisitions*, p. 125), Borges expands on this same idea, using as a starting point St Paul's verse, I Corinthians, XIII, 12: 'For now we see through a glass, darkly. . . .'

Time

Time, as we have seen, is described as being closely bound to the infinite but at the same time it forms a subject of its own. Both Sufi literature and Borges' writings refer, in various tales, to a time that has characteristics and dimensions that are different from ours and which is beyond our reach. Borges refers to a personal experience in order to 'refute' time:

'The easy thought "I am in the eighteen hundreds" ceased to be a few careless words and deepened into reality. I felt dead – I felt I was an abstract perceiver of the world. . . . No, I did not believe that I had sailed up the so-called waters of Time; rather I suspected that I was the possessor of the elusive or non-existent meaning of the inconceivable word "eternity".' (*Inquisitions*, p. 180)

Ana María Barrenechea writes:

'Time is one of the concepts that has to be disintegrated in order to destroy people's belief that they are separate entities, each with a concrete life of its own. . . .

'They are allowed to play all sorts of games: to soar up on the wings of time, to exhaust the possibilities of combining the present, the past and the future, to change the past, to turn on the endless wheel of cyclic time, to subdivide it infinitely, to detain it, to deny it, to test different hypotheses about eternity. . . .

'Borges recalls different versions of the theme of time, reduced or expanded in scope to heavenly or infernal regions: the story of the monk who thinks he has spent a minute lost in the jungle, listening to a bird singing, and when he returns discovers that everything has changed because in actual fact three hundred years have passed; the miracle of the seven young Christians of Ephesus, who hide in a cave during the persecutions by Decius, go to sleep and awake in the reign of Theodosius II (*El Aleph*, p. 90); the miracle of Mohammed, who is taken up by a mare to the Seventh Heaven, where the reverse process occurs, since he thinks he has been there a long time but when he returns to earth he picks up the water-jar which the celestial mare had overturned before the water is spilt (*Eternidad*, p. 28); the Chinese allegory of the monkey who enters the palace of the Emperor of Jade and when he returns at dawn realizes that he has lived there a year; the Chinese story of the man who watches a game of chess, at the end of which his axe is turned to ashes and centuries have elapsed; the adventure of the Dean of Santiago with Don Illan, magician of Toledo in 'The Wizard Postponed' (*Infamy*, p. 115).

'Borges, for his part, finds that these temporal lines, which are parallel but not synchronous, are an effective dissolver of the passing of time and he reproduces them in a modern context in "The Secret Miracle" (*Fictions*, p. 130). Though he first chose as an epigraph to his book the miracle of the monk and the bird, the story of Hladik more closely resembles Mohammed's experience since God grants Hladik a year of life as he faces the firing squad who are going to execute him, a year that passes between the order to fire and the obeying of this order. On the human plane, time passes only from one second to the next (compare the raindrop that glides on Hladik's cheek with the water from the jar that is about to tip over); on the miraculous plane, there is a long year filled with surprises, hopes, habits and the meticulous work of a poet.' (*Labyrinth*, pp. 143–144, 104–105)

The epigraph referred to is a quotation from the Koran, II, 261: 'And God caused him to die for a hundred years and then he revived him and said: "How long have you been here?" "A day or a part of a day", he replied.'

Time is treated in a similar way in Sufi literature. The tale of 'The Sultan who Became an Exile' (*Dervishes*, p. 35) begins with the telling of the story of Mohammed, when he was taken up into the celestial spheres by Buraq, the celestial mare. A discussion ensues among those present on the subject of time. In order to put an end to all the theoretical speculations, the Sheikh decides to convince the Sultan by means of a practical demonstration. One by one he opens and closes the windows of the audience-chamber and from them shows the Sultan impending dangers for the city; immediately afterwards he proves that these are false visions. Finally he orders a vessel of water to be brought and the Sultan is told to put his head into it for a moment. As soon as he does so, he finds himself on a deserted seashore. Thus begins a long period of seven years during which the Sultan works, gets married and undergoes various adventures. One day, when these seven years have passed and the Sultan is on the beach, he puts his hands in the water and suddenly finds himself back at the palace, as the Sultan, surrounded by the same courtiers. It is then that he realizes that only a moment has passed and that he has never really left the palace. In 'The Magic Monastery' (*Monastery*, p. 13), a group of diners undergo a similar experience.

Good and Bad

As with time and the infinite, people are not aware of all the dimensions of good and bad. Our personal judgment of good and bad comes up against a higher ethic, which has different characteristics and is referred to throughout both literatures.

'Standards of good and bad depend upon individual or group criteria, not upon objective fact.' (*Sufis*, p. 60)

The Sufis frequently illustrate the relativity of our opinions regarding good and bad. In the story of 'The Horseman and the Snake' (*Dervishes*, p. 140), a man thinks that the violent attack on him by the passing horseman is a misfortune. However, it turns out to be his salvation, since it makes him vomit the poison he has unknowingly swallowed. Something similar occurs in 'The Indian Bird' (*Dervishes*, p. 189):

' "Now you know", the bird said, "that what you thought was disaster was in fact good news for me".'

Fatima, in 'Fatima the Spinner and the Tent' (*Dervishes*, p. 72), is faced with a chain of adverse circumstances:

' "Why is it", she cried out for the third time, "that whenever I try to do something it comes to grief? Why should so many unfortunate things happen to me?" ...

'It was through these adventures that Fatima realized that what had appeared to be an unpleasant experience at the time, turned out to be an essential part of the making of her ultimate happiness.'

In the tale 'The Glance of Power' (*Wisdom*, p. 25), a dervish who leads a life of sacrifice and meditation turns out to be less advanced in the path of knowledge than a simple housewife and a scavenger, and he ends up as a disciple of these people, in order to learn humility. In 'The Man who Walked on Water' (*Dervishes*, p. 84), 'A conventionally-minded dervish, from an austerely pious school ... was absorbed in concentration upon moralistic and scholastic problems.' He hears a man mispronouncing the dervish call and he corrects him. When he turns away, full of satisfaction at having done a good deed, he discovers that this man is still making the same mistake. While he is reflecting upon the perversity of humanity and its persistence in error, he sees 'the other dervish coming towards him, walking on the surface of the water' – something which only the most advanced dervishes can do – to ask him the correct way of repeating the call, because he finds it difficult to remember it.

The tale of 'The Saint and the Sinner' (*Wisdom*, p. 91) refers specifically to the ethical field. A man who led a saintly life tried every day to correct another, who lived surrounded by vice and licentiousness. Finally both men died at the same time and, to their surprise, the decision of Divine Justice was not what either had expected. The devotee was condemned because of his arrogance and the sinner was saved because he had always valued the saint's concern about him and had regretted that, because of his evil habits, he could not please the devotee.

Borges frequently uses ethical judgments but inverts them, as for example in 'Three Versions of Judas' (*Fictions*, p. 138), 'The Theologians' (*El Aleph*, p. 37), 'Theme of the Traitor and Hero' (*Fictions*, p. 112), 'Streetcorner Man' (*Aleph*, p. 33), 'Ibn Hakkan Al-Bokhari, Dead in his Labyrinth' (*Aleph*, p. 115). Both of Borges' principal critics have pointed out the absence of fixed moral views in his writings. His characters are guided by individual ethical standards, which have nothing to do with the conventional ones of good and bad. Thus for example, when she changes men three times in one night, La Lujanera (in 'Streetcorner Man') is acting correctly for the reader, who feels that if she had remained faithful to a coward she would have shared in his guilt. And in 'The Intruder' (*Aleph*, p. 161), in the eyes of the reader the two brothers who kill the woman they share, rather than commit a crime, have made a real personal sacrifice, which is seen as an act of bravery for the sake of the noblest sentiment. Even the tortures that drive the kind Jewish writer mad and finally kill him in the concentration camp are justified and there are signs of heroism even in the attitude of the Nazi, who inwardly hates violence and feels sorry for the prisoner but believes he must forget himself, for the good of the whole nation – the man who suddenly discovers that 'it is easier to die for a religion than to live it in all its fullness' and earnestly assumes his obligation, which consists in divesting himself completely of the old man that exists in him in order to become the new man required by his times. ('Deutsches Requiem', *El Aleph*, p. 87)

Borges enjoys invalidating all preconceived and rigid standards, rescuing what is useful in the abominable and pointing out the hidden faults in the infallible. When the orthodox approach predominates, as is the case in 'The Theologians' (*El Aleph*, p. 37), where the heretic who does not share this view is burnt alive, the author ends the story by explaining that this is not of universal value:

'Aureliano realized that for the impenetrable Divinity, he and Juan de Paponia (the orthodox person and the heretic, the hater and the hated, the accuser and the accused) formed a single person.' (p. 48)

Borges presents all his theories with the same objective impartiality which enables us to view the heresy and the heretics as additional possibilities:

'During the first centuries of our era, the Gnostics fought against the Christians. They were wiped out, but we could imagine their possible victory. Had Alexandria and not Rome triumphed, the odd and dubious stories that I have summarized here would be coherent, majestic and quite common.' (*Discusión*, p. 66)

In this way Borges underlines that all our assumptions regarding heresy are relative and that truth goes beyond all men's theories. But where he completely inverts our judgment is in 'Three Versions of Judas' (*Fictions*, p. 138) when he faces us with the betrayer who has been wholly redeemed and risen to the level of divine martyrdom, with a God who takes part in the complexities of evil and misfortune which are characteristic of man.

The Quest

The theme of the quest arises as a logical consequence of the unmasking of the limitations of ordinary knowledge. This theme, which is also found in the Sufi tales, has been pointed out in Borges by Alicia Jurado. The quest that is made in books is always useless. Borges himself seems to want to prove this in the many essays and theories, the product of his literary erudition, in which he arrives at no real conclusions. In the stories 'The Library of Babel', 'The Secret Miracle' (*Fictions*, pp. 72, 130), 'Averroës' Search' (*Anthology*, p. 101) and in the poem 'The Golem' (*Anthology*, p. 77), all the attempts made by the characters to find truth in books are in vain.

'Like all the men of the Library, I have travelled in my youth, I have journeyed in search of a book, of the catalogue of catalogues, perhaps; now that my eyes can scarcely decipher what I write, I am preparing to die.' (*Fictions*, p. 72)

'A librarian wearing dark glasses asked him: "What are you looking for?" Hladik answered; "God". The librarian told him: "God is in one of the letters on one of the pages of one of the 400,000 volumes of the Clementine Library. My fathers and the fathers of my fathers have sought after that letter; I've gone blind looking for it." He removed his glasses and Hladik saw that his eyes were dead.' (*Fictions*, p. 134)

The reference to the blindness of the librarian is repeated in various tales, in the allusions to Paul Groussac (*Discusión*, p. 93) and to Borges himself, in 'The Keeper of the Books' (*Darkness*, p. 73) and also in the poem 'June, 1968' (*Darkness*, p. 71).

Borges' characters do not attain knowledge through books. The main character of 'The Anthropologist' goes seeking esoteric knowledge, which his university is interested in publishing, from certain tribes. In order to obtain it, he has to live like an Indian for over two years until he is worthy of the secrets. His experiences are authentic. When he returns, he decides not to publish his knowledge:

' "I don't really know how to tell you, but the secret means a great deal to me. Compared to it, science – our science – seems not much more than a trifle. . . . The secret, I should tell you, is not as valuable as the steps that brought me to it. Those steps have to be taken, not told." ' (*Darkness*, p. 49)

Borges describes knowledge as an individual attainment that cannot be conveyed through formal language. Generally speaking, an obsessive search, made in an area limited by preconceptions, is useless. Reason gets lost in complex labyrinths from which it cannot emerge. In 'The Garden of Forking Paths' (*Fictions*, p. 81), the descendants of Ts'ui Pen cannot find the labyrinth that he has left them despite the fact that it is facing them, nor can they understand the novel because neither coincides with their preconceived ideas of what they should be.

During his long years of confinement, the Aztec priest, in 'La Escritura del Dios', cannot decipher the Scriptures so long as he himself guides his obsessive quest. This becomes possible only when he gives up, when he realizes that 'a man gradually shapes himself into the form of his destiny; a man is, in the long run, his own circumstances. Rather than being a decipherer or an avenger, rather than being a priest of the god, I was a prisoner. From the endless labyrinth of dreams I returned to the cruel gaol as I would to my home. I blessed its dampness. . . .' (*El Aleph,* p. 122)

In 'The Argentine Writer and Tradition' (*Discusión,* p. 151), Borges admits to having searched fruitlessly for a very long time for the essential flavour of the outskirts of Buenos Aires before he found it in the writing of 'Death and the Compass' (*Fictions,* p. 117), which does not take place in Buenos Aires. 'Precisely because I had not set out to find that flavour, because I was indulging in a dream, I was able to find, after so many years, what I had previously searched for in vain.' A certain detachment is necessary for the quest. In other words, what is needed is an objective mind, free from previous and obsessive ideas.

The quest for truth is also a central theme that appears in all Sufi literature. The uselessness of information obtained from books is continually underlined. The poet Rumi says: 'The man of God is not an expert made by books'. Satires on scholars and academics are plentiful in the tales of the Mulla Nasrudin and in the book *Reflections,* by Idries Shah.

Knowledge is an individual attainment. In 'Wisdom for Sale' and 'Three Pieces of Advice' (*Dervishes,* pp. 169, 132) the uselessness of external information is underlined, as it is also in 'The Initiation of Malik Dinar' (*Dervishes,* p. 148). Malik Dinar says to himself, after many years of study, that he will go forth to seek the Hidden Teacher, but he makes a long journey by the Teacher's side without recognizing him, without realizing that he is in the presence of a great sage, who has on more than one occasion given him valuable information which he is unable to recognize or take advantage of. The quest is generally hindered and even annulled by the preconceptions and personal attachments of the seeker.

In 'Seeker after Knowledge' (*Sufis*, p. 308), the Sheikh says:

'While you live, you are learning. Those who learn through deliberate effort to learn are cutting down on the learning which is being projected upon them in the normal state. Uncultivated men often have wisdom to some degree because they allow the access of the impacts of life itself. . . . If you *try* actively to learn from them, you learn certain things, but they are predetermined things. . . . By that I mean that you are seeing what you want to see. This has become an automatic action. . . . You *cannot* judge. . . . You have set yourself a task: to find spiritual truth. You have sought this truth in the wrong directions. . . . The excessive concentration upon the theme, the anxiety and emotion which is engendered in you, will ultimately pile up to such an extent that you will seek a relief from it. . . . You will become converted to some cult which takes the responsibility. . . . The alternative, which you will not take, is detachment.'

Only after detachment from personal things takes place is the seeker in a position to find real knowledge.

Personal Renunciation

Detachment or personal renunciation, rather than ethical standards, is a requirement for knowledge which makes an objective approach possible for man. When man becomes liberated from personal desires and interests, he can see reality impartially, in other words just as it is. Borges underlines this advantage of detachment for attaining knowledge. He transcribes the point of view of an American sociologist, Veblen, which he shares, who believes that personal attachment paralyses the progress of the mind. For example, he states that the pre-eminence of the Jews in Western culture is not due to an inborn superiority, but 'because they act within this culture and at the same time do not feel tied to it by any special devotion; this is why it will always be easier for a Jew than for a non-Jewish Westerner to innovate in the Anglo-Saxon culture.' (*Discusión*, p. 160)

The theme of renunciation, which has already been dealt with in Chapter III as regards Borges' writings, is also characteristic of Sufi literature. In the story 'How Knowledge was Earned' (*Dervishes*, p. 201) we read:

'Now I can give you knowledge; for you could not have brought this carpet unless you had worked for the carpet, and not for yourself.' In the story of 'The Man with the Inexplicable Life' (*Dervishes*, p. 155), Mojud completely changes his way of life four times in order to follow the way of knowledge.

It is not an easy method because the renunciation must be sincere and inward, and not merely a matter of external behaviour. In 'The Miracle of the Royal Dervish' (*Wisdom*, p. 99), the companions of Ibrahim ben Adam wonder how he has managed to progress further on the path of knowledge in less time than they. Khidr appears and removes their doubts:

' "You gave up the expectations of security and an ordinary life. Ibrahim ben Adam was a mighty king, and threw away the sovereignty of the Sultanate of Balkh to become a Sufi. This is why he is far ahead of you. During your thirty years, too, you have gained satisfactions through renunciation itself. This has been your payment. He has always abstained from claiming any payment for his sacrifice.' Again, in 'The Golden Fortune' (*Dervishes*, p. 48) we read:

'No sooner had he divested himself of all his possessions, resigned to face whatever events life might have in store for him, than Abdul Malik saw, during his meditation-hour, a strange figure seem to rise from the floor of his room . . .

"I am your real self, which has now become almost real to you because you have done something really charitable . . . because you were able to part with your fortune without feeling personal satisfaction, I am rewarding you from the real source of reward".'

One of Malik's friends was present one day when the dervish spectre manifested itself and he was eager to obtain the same reward, so he tried to imitate Malik, but far from obtaining any gold, he fell into misfortune and disgrace.

This prerequisite of sincere renunciation is what makes the attaining of objective knowledge the result of a real inner journey.

A tale that is common to both Borges and the Sufis points out the uselessness and the negative effect of applying knowledge that has been gained in a superficial manner: A group of people obtain the formula for restoring the dead to life and decide to try it on a heap of bones they find in the desert. But as their knowledge is limited, they do not know that it is the skeleton of a wild beast, which devours them when restored to life. (*Cuentos*, p. 31 and *Dervishes*, p. 142)

The Sufis continually emphasize the need for balanced development in order to attain knowledge. A one-sided or incomplete development of certain faculties or techniques is not real knowledge but a hypertrophy of the brain. This would be the case of Funes (*Fictions*, p. 97), who, despite his capacity for seeing and remembering, 'was not very capable of thought. To think is to overlook differences, to generalize, to abstract. In Funes' overfilled world, there were nothing but details, almost contiguous details.'

In Funes' case this extraordinary attribute came about by chance, it was the result of an accident, a fortuitous event, not the result of an inner process. This accounts for the failure of mystical experiences in other tales of Borges. In 'The Aleph' (*Aleph*, p. 15), both the narrator and the ridiculous Carlos Argentino Daneri (note the poet's second name) are unable to understand nor can they fully absorb the revelation. Their lives are still tied to their former interests; the vision passes them by and the sacred object is in the hands of a fool. The narrator afterwards begins to doubt the vision. He has not reached total and objective understanding. His approach is conditioned by a neurotic passion for the dead woman and by the suspicion, jealousy and envy that Daneri inwardly arouses in him. The one person who reaches the real mystical experience is the Aztec priest, in 'La Escritura del Dios' (*El Aleph*, p. 117) who has undergone an inner evolutionary process, which has involved sincere personal renunciation.

Death of the Separated Ego and Integration in the Universal Self

Renunciation enables the individual to overcome the limitations that imprison his self and to integrate himself in a higher sphere. Borges' stories include many examples in which this is referred to either more or less explicitly. In 'The Life of Tadeo Isidoro Cruz' (*Aleph*, p. 81), when Cruz renounces his personal security, he partakes of Martín Fierro's destiny:

'He understood that his shoulder braid and his uniform were now in his way.... He understood that the other man was himself.' Judas (*Fictions*, p. 140) 'renounced honour, good, peace, the Kingdom of Heaven, as others, less heroically, renounced pleasure' and through his sacrifice, he transcends his own individuality to become identified with God. In 'The South' (*Fictions*, p. 152), when the central character draws his knife, he renounces his own life and feels that he and the South are one and the same thing; 'It was as if the South had resolved that Dahlmann should accept the duel.' The Nazi in 'Deutsches Requiem' (*El Aleph*, p. 83) says:

' "I realized however that we were on the verge of a new era which, just like the initial period of Islam or Christianity, required a new man. I hated my comrades individually; I tried in vain to reason that, for the high aim that brought us together, we were not individuals.... I suffered with him, I died with him, I have, in a way, lost myself with him; that is why I was relentless. ... Meanwhile it swung over us.... There was a feeling similar to love in the air that we breathed." ' (pp. 85, 89)

After the death of the individual takes place, he begins to talk in the plural, in other words he integrates himself into his social group. This has been referred to by Ana María Barrenechea as the dissolution of the individual and as pantheism, but she has missed the real mystical meaning, since she considers that its consequences are nihilistic and finally place man in absolute nothingness.

It really refers to the death of the separated ego, with the object of achieving a higher and permanent individuality. It is the life-giving death to which the Gospel refers:

'Verily, verily I say unto you, except a corn of wheat fall into the ground and die, it abideth alone: but if it die, it bringeth forth much fruit. He that loveth his life shall lose it; and he that hateth his life in this world shall keep it unto life eternal.' (St John, XII, 24–25) St John of the Cross and St Teresa also refer to this spiritual death, after which comes the mystical experience.

Borges' own statement, referring to one of these ecstatic experiences, has already been quoted:

'I felt dead – I felt I was an abstract perceiver of the world.... No, I did not believe that I had sailed up the so-called waters of Time; rather I suspected that I was the possessor of the elusive or non-existent meaning of the inconceivable word "eternity".' (*Inquisitions*, p. 180)

In Sufi literature as well as in Borges' writings, the mystical experience is generally viewed as integration in the universal self. Borges writes in 'La Escritura del Dios' (*El Aleph*, p. 122):

'Then, what I cannot forget nor convey happened. The union with Divinity, with the universe (I do not know whether these words are different) took place.... I saw a very high wheel, which was not facing me, nor was it behind me, nor at my sides, but everywhere at the same time. This wheel was made of water but also of fire and it was infinite (though only the edge could be seen). It was made up of all things that will be, that are and that have been, all interwoven, and I was one of the threads of that complete weft, and Pedro de Alvarado, who tormented me, was another. All the causes and effects were there and I had only to look at that wheel to understand it all, without end.

'Whoever has glimpsed the universe, whoever has glimpsed the ardent purposes of the universe, cannot think of one man and of his trivial moments of happiness or misfortune, even though that man be himself. That man *has been himself* and now he does not care. What does he care about that man's fate, about that man's nation, if he is now nobody?' And again in 'The Aleph' (*Aleph*, p. 15):

'I saw the teeming sea; I saw daybreak and nightfall; I saw the multitudes of America; I saw a silvery cobweb in the centre of a black pyramid ... I saw bunches of grapes, snow, tobacco, lodes of metal, steam; I saw convex equatorial deserts and each one of their grains of sand ... I saw a sunset in Querétaro that seemed to reflect the colour of a rose in Bengal ... I saw my own face and my own bowels; I saw your face; and I felt dizzy....' (pp. 27, 28)

This integration in the universal self, when it refers to the mystical experience, is characteristic of Sufi literature. Borges

himself provides an example, taken from the Sufi mystic Faridudin Attar's 'Parliament of the Birds', with which he seems to be
obsessed, judging by the repeated references to it made throughout
his work.

'The remote king of the birds, the Simurgh, lets fall a mag-
nificent feather in the middle of China and the birds decide to
look for him, because they are tired of their unending anarchy.
They know that the name of the king means thirty birds, they
know that they will find him in Kaf, the circular mountain that
surrounds the earth. They undertake the almost infinite adventure; they traverse seven valleys or seas; the sixth valley is called
the Valley of Astonishment, the last one is the Valley of Death.
Many of the pilgrims give up and others die. Thirty of them,
who have been purified by their work, reach the mountain of the
Simurgh. They finally see it and realize that they are the Simurgh
and that the Simurgh is each one and all of them.' (*Eternidad*,
p. 144)

Jalaludin Rumi, one of the greatest Sufi poets, says:
'The two-and-seventy creeds and sects in the world
Do not really exist: I swear by God that every creed and sect
– 'tis I.
Earth and air and water and fire, nay, body and soul too –
'tis I.
Truth and falsehood, good and evil, ease and difficulty from
first to last.
Knowledge and learning and asceticism and piety and faith
– 'tis I.
The fire of Hell, be assured, with its flaming limbos,
Yes, and Paradise and Eden and the Houris – 'tis I.
This earth and heaven with all they hold,
Angels, Peris, Genies and Mankind – 'tis I.' (*Sufis*, p. 27)
In 'The Tale of the Sands' (*Dervishes*, p. 23), the stream was
convinced that it was its destiny to cross the desert, but there was
no way. The sands said:
' "By hurtling in your own accustomed way you cannot get
across. You will either disappear or become a marsh. You must
allow the wind to carry you over, to your destination ... by allow-
ing yourself to be absorbed in the wind.'

'This idea was not acceptable to the stream. After all, it had never been absorbed before. It did not want to lose its individuality.' But it was only when the stream raised its vapour into the arms of the wind, letting itself fall again as rain, that it was able to say:

' "Yes, now I have learned my true identity." '

The Extraordinary

Mystical experiences and the elimination of time are not the only extraordinary elements found both in Sufi literature and in Borges' work. The Sufis repeatedly refer to miracles carried out by their mystical teachers of the past or else they use ancient teaching stories such as those of 'The Arabian Nights', in which the typical Oriental magic is present. Borges also shows interest in these miraculous phenomena and it would seem that he searched for them in all his readings, since he frequently quotes or reproduces them. His *Cuentos Breves y Extraordinarios*, written in collaboration with Adolfo Bioy Casares, includes a complete collection; none of the supernatural elements that are plentiful in Sufi literature are missing: talismans, imprisoned genies, ogres, omens, split personalities, seers, levitation and all kinds of miraculous happenings.

Many of Borges' characters have extraordinary faculties. Those of 'The Aleph', 'The Zahir' (*Anthology*, pp. 138, 128) and 'La Escritura del Dios' (*El Aleph*, p. 117) survive the fantastic experience of the mystical vision. Funes (*Fictions*, p. 97) is capable of simultaneously embracing all things, in all their fullness, without omitting the smallest detail of anything that he is faced with, and registering it all in his memory for ever. In 'The Circular Ruins', 'Tlön, Uqbar, Orbis Tertius' (*Fictions*, pp. 52, 17) and 'The Golem' (*Anthology*, p. 77), mere products of the human mind come to life. The central character of 'The Immortal' (*El Aleph*, p. 7) tells of his survival through the ages, in various reincarnations. In 'His End and his Beginning' (*Darkness*, p. 117) 'A Theologian in Death' (*Infamy*, p. 103) and 'The Theologians' (*El Aleph*, p. 37) Borges introduces the central character after his death. In 'The Secret Miracle' (*Fictions*, p. 130), 'The Wizard Postponed' (*Infamy*, p. 115), 'The Flower of Coleridge' (*Inquisi-*

tions, p. 10) and 'The Other Death' (*Aleph*, p. 103) the course of time is altered. In 'The Aleph' (*Aleph*, p. 15) and 'The Chamber of Statues' (*Infamy*, p. 107) reference is made to objects that can make the most surprising revelations. In 'Tale of the Two Dreamers' (*Infamy*, p. 111) and 'The Dream of Coleridge' (*Inquisitions*, p. 14) telepathic messages are transmitted through sleep. Most of these unnatural phenomena are repeated in his essays.

References to 'The Arabian Nights' are repeated in a really obsessive manner throughout Borges' work, they form a kind of 'leit motiv'. However, the similarities between the Arabian tales and Borges' writings are only external. 'The Arabian Nights', like most Oriental literature, is enveloped in an atmosphere of remoteness. The exotic atmosphere and the fantastic elements, though picturesque, are totally disconnected from our reality. In spite of this, the controversy aroused by Borges' work and the critiques of Sufi books prove the impact of both on the reader.

The Sufis say that the versions of this ancient collection of stories known to the West lack all their original strength, because the translators were ignorant of the true essence of the Oriental teaching story: its inner content. Borges somehow managed to revive the ancient legends, which have a similar effect to that of the Sufi tales, and he captured this magical and hypnotic atmosphere, assimilating it in his own way. This is why Borges' writings differ from fantastic literature in general, because far from helping the reader to escape from reality, they bring him face to face with his duty towards the transcendental and with his own ignorance and limitations.

V
Coincidences in the Literary Techniques

Neither Borges nor the Sufis wish to convey literal truths, since their objective is to produce certain effects on the reader, and the most important coincidences between them can probably be found in the techniques and formal procedures they use to achieve this; this would indicate that they begin from a viewpoint that is analogous to reality.

As regards Sufism, there is no doubt that the main object of the technique is to develop the mind and prepare it for a higher level of knowledge. Idries Shah replies to a self-styled seeker after knowledge:

'You say you have come to seek. I have nothing to give you except the way to understand how to seek – but you think that you can already do that.' (*Reflections*, p. 69)

'By its very construction, Sufism cannot be preached. It does not rely upon undermining other systems and offering a substitute, or a more plausible one.' (*Sufis*, p. 91)

'Sufism relies upon the composite impact – the "scatter" dissemination.' (*Sufis*, p. 91)

Sufism tries to bridge the gap between the ordinary mental state and another state, to enable man to reach a level which, in the first state, is completely beyond his reach. The need is akin to that of a child who, before fully understanding abstract numbers, needs a previous stage which prepares him by means of analogies using different numbers of concrete objects.

Various Levels of Interpretation of the Same Material

Sufi literature is constructed on various levels for this reason.

'The net effect of experiencing a tale at several different levels at once is to awaken the innate capacity for understanding on a comprehensive, more objective . . . way of thinking.' (*Sufis*, p. 92)

'The Sufi seeker will learn, at one and the same time, several different things, at their own levels of perception and potentiality. This is another difference between Sufism and the systems which rest on the assumption that only one thing is being learned at any one moment.' (*Sufis*, p. 78)

The Sufis give us very few explanations of their tales but with these few we can discover aspects that we had ignored in general during the first reading. Most of these explanations can be found in 'The Subtleties of Mulla Nasrudin' (*Sufis*, pp. 56–97). Apart from the joke and the moral, these tales can be viewed from different perspectives and considered separately or else experienced concurrently and transposed into other fields, through the 'total yet composite impact of the Sufi tale'. The tales sometimes refer to another level of interpretation, using technical terms that can be substituted for homonyms, thus leading the story into deeper areas than the apparent ones. In such cases much of the impact of a tale may be lost in the translation, as has happened with the story of the donkey and its load of salt and of wool (p. 64). Some Sufis take advantage of a characteristic of the Semitic languages, in which words are constructed by means of a consonantal group; by changing the vowels, the same group of consonants can have various meanings. The cryptographic procedures which strongly appeal to Borges and which he refers to in 'A Vindication of the Cabala' (*Discusión*, p. 55) are based on these possibilities of substitution and on adding up the numerical equivalents for the letters.

Sometimes even in the external formulation a tale has different meanings, as for example the story of the Mulla looking for bird's eggs in a last year's nest (*Sufis*, p. 88)

'The fact that this joke can be read in at least two ways might deter the formalist thinker, but provides the dervish with the opportunity of understanding the duality of real being, which is obscured by conventional human thinking. Hence what is its absurdity to the intellectual becomes its strength to the intuitively perceptive.' (*Sufis*, p. 89)

When Borges says 'lasting works are always capable of a rich and endless ambiguity', he is referring to the search for a language capable of producing multiple effects. Both his critics underline this characteristic of his books and Borges himself confirms it in the 'Prologue to Artifices' (*Fictions*, p. 95) when, referring to 'The South', he writes 'it is perhaps my best tale, and I need only warn the reader that it can be read as a narration of fictional events or in another way.' In the 'Prologue to the Garden of Forking Paths' (*Fictions*, p. 13), he states: 'The Babylon Lottery' (*Fictions*, p. 59) is not totally innocent of symbolism' and he gives a few clues to interpret 'The Library of Babel' (*Fictions*, p. 72) and other stories.

On this point, Alicia Jurado explains that, among other meanings, 'The Babylon Lottery' can be seen as a prediction of the country's future.

'Everything that Borges writes is of interest to the reader because it makes him use his intelligence, and the more cultured the reader, the more he enjoys Borges; there are frequent literary, historical or philosophical references, and the perception of them by the reader gives him the added pleasure of solving a puzzle placed at random in the text ... (for instance) recognizing Shakespeare in the man who knew 'little Latin and less Greek', or the etymological meaning of 'poet' in 'The Maker' (*Dreamtigers*, p. 22).' (*Genio*, p. 110)

Ana María Barrenechea specially analyses those tales of Borges which contain keys:

'Perhaps it would be an exaggeration to link the kind of tales that attract Borges to the idea of the secret key to the universe. The tales we are referring to are those that describe some events and give clues of other possible interpretations, which the discerning reader discovers as he reads on, but which are not actually revealed until right at the end of the story. . . .

'In 'Tlön, Uqbar, Orbis Tertius' (*Fictions*, p. 17) there is the discussion with Bioy Casares of a tale written in the first person with clues "which would enable a few readers – a very few – to guess the atrocious and banal reality." But he then does something even more complex. In 'Theme of the Traitor and Hero' (*Fictions*, p. 112) he incorporates the task of his readers with the plot, because he relies on the skill of him who traces the truth through Kilpatrick's published history, which was hidden or only partly revealed, perhaps intentionally.... Ryan suspects that the author included them so that somebody in the future would get to the truth.

'We could conclude that Borges is guided by an aesthetic interest only.... However, there would seem to be another deeper motivation, apart from this one ... yet another description of man's insecurity regarding the key to the universe and a vague, pantheistic reference to the uniting of completely opposite destinies. Perhaps Tlön's sentence regarding an event that can be both atrocious and banal will help strengthen the idea of the double interpretation ...

'The author's own tales are often aimed at the useless attempt to understand a Divine message, when we do not know what is fundamental and what is incidental.' (*Labyrinth*, pp. 74–76)

Mixture of Various Levels in the Narrative

Different planes of reality are also included in the structure of the tale to achieve a more comprehensive and complex approach to it and to create confusion regarding the limits of reality, and thus cast doubt on these limits.

Borges is attracted by tales within a tale, like 'The Arabian Nights' and he creates fiction with this characteristic. Ana María Barrenechea comments:

'The story of Tlön is an attempt to insert an imaginary world on earth, thought up by a group of people, until, by dint of thinking about it, the fantastic orb becomes substantial and sends objects made of strange materials to earth: a compass and a metal cone. The author inserts a second plane of unreality – within the fantastic orb which becomes real – which he also wishes to make real, that of the duplication of *hrönir*.... A tale with a Chinese box structure: unreal worlds lying one within the other and at the same time within this world which disintegrates on contact with such phantasmagorias.

'The plane of life, the plane of literary fiction, of dreams, of spells, the plane of the supernatural and the Divine, all contradicting one another, until finally we wonder whether we are real beings or shadows.' (*Labyrinth*, pp. 38, 39)

Borges is quite aware of the effect of this artifice, since he analyses it in 'Translators of the Thousand and One Nights' (*Eternidad*, p. 99) and 'Partial Enchantments of the *Quixote*' (*Inquisitions*, p. 43).

'Cervantes could not have had recourse to amulets or sorcery, but he insinuated the supernatural in a subtle and therefore more effective way.... Cervantes delights in fusing the objective and the subjective, the world of the reader and the world of the book....

'I believe I have found the answer: those inversions suggest that if the characters in a story can be readers or spectators, then we, their readers or spectators, can be fictitious.' (*Inquisitions*, pp. 43–46)

There are many other Sufi tales, apart from the 'Arabian Nights', with this characteristic. In the story of 'The Sultan who Became an Exile' (*Dervishes*, p. 45), the plane on which the initial literary fiction takes place seems more real to us with the telling of the legend. But once the audience-chamber becomes the setting for so many miraculous visions, it turns into a supernatural setting rather than a fictional one. In contrast to this magical plane, the seashore to which the Sultan is suddenly transported seems absolutely normal and real, to the extent that we take this to be the Sultan's real situation and in the end we are surprised by his sudden return to the original setting, which we had completely forgotten. Thus, paradoxically, the plane of the Sultan's real reality becomes unreal by means of the disintegrating effect of mixing the magical plane with the real one, which is what happens in this tale. The literary plane, the legendary plane and the magical plane are successively included in each other, until our rational minds become confused and are freed from the barriers that limit and restrict their working.

All the supernatural elements in Sufi literature are closely linked to the plane of reality since they are generally referred to as faculties of teachers of the past, who are described as simple human beings with greater wisdom. By mixing the most incredible phenomena with ordinary events and by describing them as the working of human faculties, they are made to seem less extraordinary.

Ana María Barrenechea points out that Borges was aware of the effect of mixing reality with fantasy:

'When analyzing his fantastic tales (Borges) has insisted that they require some concrete element to give them a touch of reality. The reality of Adolfo Bioy Casares, Alfonso Reyes, Ezequiel Martínes Estrada and Enrique Amorín shores up the fantasy of Tlön, the reality of Philip Guedalla, the fantasy of the inventor of Al-Mu'tasim; likewise Patricio Gannon that of Pedro Damián, the stallholder, and Pedro Henríquez Ureña that of the Zahir. . . .

'The author's own reality thus forms part of the multiplicity of fictional experiences and lends them the support of his existence while he for his part allows himself to be imbued with the mystery.' (*Labyrinth*, p. 127) In this way, by mixing reality with fantasy, Borges makes our apparently concrete world unreal and transforms the unreal and magical world into a real one. This is probably more than a game of literary effects. Just as Borges tries to make us doubt what we think is real, he is probably also trying to point out to us the real existence of certain phenomena which we assume are recognized today in our Western culture because it has created a new branch of learning called parapsychology to study them scientifically.

Mystery

Leaving certain elements veiled with mystery in the narrative is another procedure that manages to confuse our limited and rational minds, which are used to arriving at simple conjectures based on only a few elements of something which is really extremely complex and difficult to understand fully. The Sufi story 'The Ancient Coffer of Nuri Bey' (*Dervishes*, p. 31) clearly illustrates this confusing and disturbing effect on the reader:

'Nuri Bey was a reflective and respected Albanian, who had married a wife much younger than himself.

One evening when he had returned home earlier than usual, a faithful servant came to him and said:

"Your wife, our mistress, is acting suspiciously.

She is in her apartments with a huge chest, large enough to hold a man, which belonged to your grandmother.

It should contain only a few ancient embroideries.
I believe that there may now be much more in it.
She will not allow me, your oldest retainer, to look inside."
Nuri went to his wife's room, and found her sitting discon-
solately beside the massive wooden box.
"Will you show me what is in the chest?" he asked.
"Because of the suspicion of a servant, or because you do not
trust me?"
"Would it not be easier just to open it, without thinking about
the undertones?" asked Nuri.
"I do not think it possible."
"Is it locked?"
"Yes."
"Where is the key?"
She held it up, "Dismiss the servant and I will give it to you."
The servant was dismissed. The woman handed over the key
and herself withdrew, obviously troubled in mind.
Nuri Bey thought for a long time. Then he called four gardeners
from his estate. Together they carried the chest by night unopened
to a distant part of the grounds, and buried it.
The matter was never referred to again.'
Often Borges faces us with events that have nothing to do with
the plot, without giving us any explanations. Thus he lets the
reader arrive at his own conclusions. The reader is at a loss because of his mental habits which are inadequate for arriving at an
explanation without a reference point on which to build the customary logical conjectures that satisfy him. Using mystery, Borges
faces us with the infinite possibilities that are inherent in the
complex panorama which, just like real reality, is beyond our
reach, and he obliges us to make an extraordinary effort to absorb
it. He asserts that 'the solution to the mystery is always inferior
to the mystery itself', and Harss describes this procedure as one of
his greatest achievements, exceeding perhaps those of all our
present writers.
This technique can be found in many of his tales but the impact
is perhaps strongest in 'The Anthropologist', from his most recent
book, *In Praise of Darkness* (p. 47). At the university the anthropologist has been advised to study the esoteric rites that still exist

in certain tribes in the West. His professor suggested that he should go and live on an Indian reservation, that he should observe the rites and discover the secret that was revealed by the medicine-men to initiates. On his return, he would prepare a thesis which the university would publish. 'For over two years he lived on the prairie, in the tents or out in the open . . . he even dreamed in a language that was not the language of his fathers.' He finally discovered the secret, but when he returned to the city, 'he made his way to his professor's office and told him that he now knew the secret and that he had made up his mind not to reveal it. . . . "I don't really know how to tell you, but the secret means a great deal to me. Compared to it, science – our science – seems not much more than a trifle. . . . The secret, I should tell you, is not as valuable as the steps that brought me to it. Those steps have to be taken, not told." ' (pp. 47, 49) Thus the secret remains a mystery, a mystery intensified by the insidious suggestion the author makes at the end, that he and the anthropologist are the same person: '(he) married, was divorced, and is now a librarian at Yale'. Through this sentence the original description of the anthropologist is also seen in a new light and could coincide with that of Borges.

The fact that Borges communicates his own bewilderment and uncertainty and that therefore he shares these feelings with us is comforting. But the suspicion that he knows, that he has the solution to the mystery and that he does not wish to reveal it, is tormenting. This is the same disturbing feeling that the reader gets when reading Sufi tales, in which the teacher knows but cannot transmit the knowledge – nor does he want to, because each person has to follow the path on his own.

Various Possible Simultaneous Viewpoints

In 'The Approach to Al-Mu'tasim' (*Fictions*, p. 35), after the mysterious ending, Borges puts forward various hypotheses as possible solutions which, far from clarifying the mystery, confuse one even more than the mystery itself does. The simultaneous development of various possible theories on one single subject makes us abandon our customary one-sided approach in order to cover a more complex field. The fact that all the approaches seem to be possible means that their strength is mutually annulled and in the end one infers that truth is beyond all these possible partial approaches, in other words, it remains beyond our reach.

This is at any rate the effect it produces on the tea seekers in 'The Story of Tea' (*Dervishes*, p. 88), because they have been given so many possible and different definitions of tea.

'The greatest philosopher of Anja ('there') collected all the information he could about tea, and concluded that it must be a substance which existed but rarely, and was of another order than anything then known. For was it not referred to as being a herb, a water, green, black, sometimes bitter, sometimes sweet?'

In the story 'The Cure of Human Blood' (*Dervishes*, p. 96), the outcome immediately produces a string of interpretations. Some concluded that the King had been rewarded for his good action. Others attributed his improvement to the relief of the mothers and children, acting upon Divine power. The Byzantines thought that he was healed in response to the holy prayers of the clergy. The Sufi El-Arif said that 'it was his single-mindedness coupled with the constructive desires of the mothers who wanted a remission of the disease'. El-Ghazali said: 'An effect can take place only through a manner devised to operate within the time allotted to its attainment'.

There are various short but clear examples in *Reflections* of the limitations of any one-sided interpretation of a complex fact.

'(Man) seeks simple answers for simple questions. There is no simple answer to . . . "What makes that car travel?"

'The answer "Petrol" is as true, untrue and incomplete and probably useless, as the answer, "The driver, the sparking-plugs, the wheels, the transmission and so on".' (p. 128)

All Borges' essays, whether philosophical, literary or religious, follow this procedure. Alicia Jurado in particular analyses it in this way:

'The Chinese emperor who constructs the famous wall is also the one who orders that all books written before his time should be burnt. Borges decides to find a reason to explain both facts and he uses the characteristic procedure. The first hypothesis is magical, the second one, dramatic, . . . the third, literary. . . . According to the fourth hypothesis, the emperor is a philosopher. . . . In the fifth, he is a moralist. . . . The sixth and last hypothesis resorts to impenetrable Divinity.... Finally, he imagines that the virtue of all forms is in the form itself and not in the conjectural content and he ends up with the following suggestion: "Music, states of happiness, mythology, faces moulded by time, certain twilights and certain places – all these are trying to tell us something, or have told us something we should not have missed, or are about to tell us something: that imminence of a revelation that is not yet produced is, perhaps the aesthetic reality." (*Inquisitions*, p. 5)

'I have included this essay to give an idea of Borges' fertile imagination. To exhaust the possible interpretations of an event, to trace the various forms that a legend, a metaphor, a philosophical doctrine or a poetic idea can adopt: these are the exercises that he prefers.' (*Genio*, pp. 122, 123)

Ana María Barrenechea in turn states:

'The author sometimes proposes two or more interpretations for an event, all of which are plausible, and suggests implicitly that they are perhaps all true simultaneously, because reality and especially human psychology are complex....

'If we analyse Borges' prose syntactically, we discover a vast region which could be described as the doubt and conjecture style ... full of explanations, adverbs of doubt, subjunctives, that reveal attitudes ranging from total ignorance to a certainty which always draws attention to the fallacious elements in human certainty. Thus, behind the words, there remains a world in which nothing is certain and there is nothing which can be used as a basis to lean on. Above all, what remains is an author who is convinced about the uncertain nature of the universe and the problems involved in attaining knowledge about mankind.

'Borges sometimes adds a warning, between commas or parentheses to the main sentence, on the subjective nature of all human assertions.... What is fundamental is to convey that all assertions are not a direct transcription of reality but the version given by an individual and therefore fallible: "until I noticed, or thought I noticed, an implicit or esoteric plot beneath the apparent one" ... "they believed (or thought that they believed)".

'Through these (parenthetical constructions and expressions of doubt and conjecture) the author expresses both the difficulties in interpreting a reality which is fleeting and the wish to show us, humbly but with the utmost rigour, the precariousness of our knowledge. Ultimately he conveys uncertainty and phantasmagoria while seeking heedfulness and precision.' (*Labyrinth*, pp. 138, 136, 139, 143, 142)

This brings us to the procedure that is most widely used in both the literatures we are discussing.

The Contrast

The Sufis consider this procedure to be one of the bases of their teaching.

'The working together of opposite things is another significant theme of Sufism. When apparent opposites are reconciled, the individuality is not only complete, it also transcends the bounds of ordinary humanity as we understand them.'

'The Sufi doctrine of equipoise between extremes has several meanings. Where it applies to discipleship, the capacity to learn from another, it means that the individual must be free from incorrect thinking before he can start to learn. Our Western would-be disciple has to learn that he cannot bring his assumptions about his own capacity to learn into a field where he does not in fact know what it is that he is trying to learn. . . .

'Similarly, the opposite extreme – the man who wants to submit himself completely to the will of a master – which is said to be characteristic of the Eastern mind, is next to useless. The Seeker must first attain some measure of balance between these two extremes before he can be said to have the capacity to learn.' (*Sufis*, pp. 126, 315)

This underlines the extraordinary nature of this teaching, which calls a physical law a doctrine that serves to explain certain psychological mechanisms on which many of the teaching techniques are based. The Sufis assert: 'Two apparently opposite things can inwardly work together.' The object of the contrast procedures is obviously to complete and balance the working of the mind. They generally act as correctives, as is pointed out in the following example from *Reflections* (p. 29).

'Try to remember, as a corrective against automatic assumptions, the story of the wise dervish and the mother.

A woman was carrying a baby down a hill when she saw what looked like a reverend dervish, and she asked him to bless her child. He immediately started to curse it.

This made her weep bitterly, and regard the man as utterly evil.

What she did not know about him was that he belonged to a realm where things always went by contraries.'

Two contrary elements can have a compensatory effect, in other words, both extremes remain on the same plane. Generally speaking, both extremes are wrong but they lead us to a happy medium, as in the examples:

'People who think that they know all are often insufferable – rather like those who imagine that they know nothing.' (*Reflections*, p. 34)

'Whoever says everything is true is a fool, whoever says all is untrue is a liar.' (*Caravan*, p. 80)

The contrast technique is also one of the main characteristics of Borges' writings. In 'Theme of the Traitor and Hero' (*Fictions*, p. 112), the contrast has a double, compensatory effect. First, the person who was regarded as a hero turns out to be a traitor. But his treachery is finally compensated by his co-operative efforts in trying to transform his own death into an incentive for the revolutionaries. The result is a happy medium in which Kilpatrick is neither the hero people think he is nor the unforgivable traitor who must die, but an ordinary man.

Borges obliges us to overcome our limitations by developing two simultaneous and contrary ideas and representing a more complex view of reality, such as he proposes in the ideal world described in 'Tlön, Uqbar, Orbis Tertius' (*Fictions*, p. 17).

'Philosophical books invariably contain thesis and antithesis, the strict pros and cons of a doctrine. A book that does not contain its opposite, or 'counter-book', is considered incomplete.' (p. 28) He also refers to this procedure, which he justifies by calling it an educational technique, in his essay 'Two Books' (*Inquisitions*, p. 129).

Luís Harss says:

'He gives us contradictory explanations of events, without favouring any, and simply contrasts them, opposing the thesis to the antithesis in order to obtain a dramatic synthesis.' (*Mainstream*, p. 122) And according to Ana María Barrenechea, often Borges 'proposes an opposite interpretation and by leaving both versions in the story in this way, the violence of their encounter brings out the value of the tale.' (*Labyrinth*, p. 142)

In many cases Borges leads us to the end of the story with a conventional and false or incomplete approach and then he suddenly surprises us with a totally opposite outcome, which is accentuated by the juxtaposition. Our verbal and logical minds are shocked by the unexpected ending which makes us abandon the rigid patterns of our thoughts and sensations. For example, in 'Streetcorner Man' (*Infamy*, p. 87), when we discover right at the end that the harmless and mediocre narrator is the man who has avenged the whole neighbourhood, we are completely confused and we realize that our first reading and interpretation was faulty; we therefore have to retrace our thoughts and find a parallel approach to explain the other ending, which we had not foreseen.

The endings of 'Emma Zunz' (*El Aleph*, p. 61), 'Death and the Compass' (*Fictions*, p. 117) and 'The Form of the Sword' (*Fictions*, p. 106) have a disturbing effect on us because they prove that appearances are very easily deceptive. The effect is even greater in the case of contrasting crossed endings, as in 'The Theologians' (*El Aleph*, p. 37) and 'Three Versions of Judas' (*Fictions*, p. 138). The effect of this unexpected last moment shock transcends the fictional plane and has a direct impact on the reader, who generally becomes involved in it.

This effect was deliberately aimed at in the baroque theatre in Spain, where it was also accentuated by means of crossed themes and double and contrary endings, with a didactic-religious or political purpose, as Joaquín Casualdero points out in his studies of the Spanish theatre. (*Estudios sobre el teatro español*)

In Sufi literature these contrasts are also used to bring out the second element in a story. In 'The Dervish and the Princess' and 'The Gnat Namouss – and the Elephant' (*Dervishes*, pp. 194, 58), the intensifying effect of this second element increases the distance that exists between reality and mere subjective opinion. There are also tales in which the crossed endings produce a double effect, as in Borges' tales. In the tale 'The Saint and the Sinner' (*Wisdom*, p. 91), a devotee tries to convert a libertine. At the outcome, we discover much to our surprise that, when the moment comes for them to be judged, the saint is condemned because of his haughtiness and the sinner is saved because of his humility.

A large number of the brief meditations found in *Reflections* have this antithetical construction which gives emphasis to the ending.

'Knowledge is something which you can use.

Belief is something which uses you.' (p. 125)

'People used to play with toys.

Now the toys play with them.' (p. 145)

The strength of the impact of the second opposing element on the reader is generally used as a stimulus to produce the opposite effect.

'A pungent thought is a corrective to deterioration of the thinking: like cold water helping slack muscles to work again. If you dislike the thought more than the sting of a shower which stimulates, and you do not feel its regenerating power – prepare for your mental obesity to possess you completely: it won't be long now.' (p. 125)

I think Borges' insidious and pungent comments, which so upset certain readers, have a similar aim, since the people who are most put out by the author's statements are precisely those who pigeonhole and restrict reality. The unbiased reader will not find in his words anything more than a game, played by someone who is not really against any particular faction but all of them, since his truth is beyond all superficial human divisions, on a plane that transcends them. The unbiased reader will discover humour in his words, used simply as a technique. Borges proves to be quite aware of this technique in his essay 'The Art of Insult' (*Eternidad*, p. 119). We thus arrive at another procedure which connects Borges' writing with Sufi literature.

Humour

Humour is yet another baffling aspect of Sufism. A Westerner would never associate humour with a metaphysical quest or a mystical teaching. However in 'The Art of Insult', Borges refers to the satirical elements, linking them with the other characteristics of his own work and of Sufi literature which have been outlined.

*The Search for a Striking and Non-rational Language Viewed
as a Mere Technique*

Satire, according to Borges, 'is derived from the magical
curses of fury, not from reasoning. It is a relic of the unlikely
state in which an injury inflicted on a name falls upon the possessor of that name.' (*Eternidad*, p. 151)

'Whenever an enquiry was made concerning a certain auctioneer,
who was more of an orator, someone would be sure to say that he
was busy knocking down *The Divine Comedy*. The epigram is
not stunningly clever but the mechanism is typical. It is a case (as
with all epigrams) of a misleading confusion of ideas.... The
listener accepts the argument without hesitation because it is not
put to him as an argument.' (*Eternidad*, p. 148)

The Relative Value of Words

In 'The Art of Insult' (*Eternidad*, p. 145) we read:
'The satirist proceeds with the greatest vigilance, but with the
vigilance of the card-sharper who is aware of the fictitious nature
of the cards, with their corruptible sky bespangled with two-faced
people. Three kings win the day in poker but they mean nothing
in "truco" (a Spanish card-game).'

The Didactic Value Hidden in Books

Swift, who had an essentially bitter nature, intended to slander
the human race with his account of Gulliver's travels, as Borges
comments in 'The Art of Insult':

'The first (journeys, to Liliput and Brobdingnag) come nowhere
near the complexities of our own existence, its fire and its algebra.
The third, the most amusing one, pokes fun at experimental
science, using the well-known procedure of inversion: Swift's
delapidated laboratories seek to breed sheep without wool, to use
ice to make gunpowder, to soften marble for making cushions.'
(p. 152)

The Effect of Contraries

Borges analyses the procedure in various famous satires, which
consist in accompanying the original element of judgment with
another in opposition to it, thus counteracting their effect and

making them seem ridiculous. Again from 'The Art of Insult':

'One of the satirical traditions (which was not neglected by Macedonio Fernández, Quevedo nor Bernard Shaw) is the unconditional reversing of terms. According to this famous recipe, the doctor is inevitably accused of preaching contamination and death, the notary of stealing, the executioner of encouraging longevity, works of fiction of sending the reader to sleep or petrifying him....' (p. 148)

'Groussac, in that good ill-humour of his, complies with the most rigorous ritual of the satirical game. He pretends that the mistakes of his opponents distress him . . . he uses laudatory words to attack....' (p. 150)

Various critics have pointed out the humour in Borges' writings although they have not analysed it thoroughly. Luís Harss lays emphasis on his sense of humour and Alicia Jurado says, when stating the conditions his audience must fulfil:

'Borges is a writer for intelligent, well-informed and sensitive men and women, who have the necessary sense of humour.' (*Genio*, p. 55)

'I would like to refer to some of Borges' stories which are of a different kind and which have received very little attention, so far as I know. These are the humorous tales which he wrote together with Adolfo Bioy Casares.... The fact that they were written under a pen name enabled him to abandon all inhibitions and give free rein to his sense of humour. 'Six Problems for Don Isidro Parodi' are a set of highly improbable detective stories.... Through the whole book there runs a festive note, a satire devoid of bitterness, humour of an extremely intelligent kind.' (*Genio*, pp. 55, 128, 130)

Ana María Barrenechea in turn says in her Conclusion:

'Moreover we see him pass to and fro from the lucidity of an intelligence that is aware of human limitations to one that indulges in all the games of irony and scepticism and to the passion of one who is deeply moved by his destiny, which is that of a man lost in the universe. His jokes can produce farcical situations but they never lose their basic seriousness.' (*Labyrinth*, p. 144)

In actual fact there is humour in almost all of Borges' works. It co-exists, hidden behind his literary erudition and the quest for truth in his essays. It can be found in his tales that have a metaphysical theme, in the marginal notes, in ironic comments and even in some of his experiences of a mystical nature. But where it most resembles the Oriental tale, which contains deeper meanings behind the joke, is perhaps in *Cuentos Breves y Extraordinarios,* written in collaboration with Adolfo Bioy Casares.

Humour is also a characteristic technique in Sufi literature. When Idries Shah revealed not long ago the existence of a collection of jokes designed to transmit higher knowledge, he confused more than one serious investigator. However, humour is a procedure that fits in perfectly with Sufi characteristics, since it is eminently practical rather than theoretical, and is intended to free the mind from all the adhesions of rigid thinking.

'The Legend of Nasrudin' (*Thinkers,* p. 191) dating from at least the thirteenth century, touches on some of the reasons for introducing Nasrudin and for the humorous character of the tales. Humour cannot be prevented from spreading; it has a way of slipping through the patterns of thought which are imposed upon mankind by habit and design. This can be seen from the fact that such diverse and alien organizations as the British Society for the Promotion of Christian Knowledge and the Soviet Government have both pressed Nasrudin into service. Turkey, through its information department, has published a selection of the metaphysical jokes attributed to this supposedly Moslem preacher who is the archetype of the Sufi mystic. And yet the dervish orders were suppressed by law in republican Turkey.

Nobody really knows who Nasrudin was, where he lived or when. This is truly in character, for the whole intention is to provide a figure who cannot really be characterized and who is timeless.

'The Mulla is variously referred to as very stupid, improbably clever, the possessor of mystical secrets. The dervishes use him as a figure to illustrate, in their teachings, the antics characteristic of the human mind.' (*Exploits,* p. 11)

The Mulla is probably the most versatile and resilient character in Sufi literature, because of the possibilities offered him by humour. He undergoes the most unusual changes in his stories. He has all the faults and virtues of mankind, including those that are mutually contradictory. This is where the strength of his impact lies, with which he destroys all the pigeon-holing mechanisms that our minds are used to employing. The Mulla's actions are always unpredictable for the reader who is inevitably confused and tries to puzzle out the meaning of such unusual reactions. But the Mulla is not the only example of humour in Sufi literature, since there is humour in a great number of the tales and in most of the reflections that are so plentiful in Sufi books.

VI
Conclusions

From the point of view put forward in this book, Borges' work contains an important and complete message for present day man, which covers the socio-political, psychological, philosophical, and even the religious area, and counteracts the widespread versions according to which Borges' writing is just a frivolous game or is simply exceptional prose or leads to a frozen destiny.

From a socio-political point of view Borges confuses the Argentines, because he is the only writer who does not limit himself to our frontiers when approaching reality, but covers the world panorama and postulates universalism. I do not intend to prove that he is right here, nor to list the reasons that would explain his point of view, but only to state that his is not the Utopian alchemy of one who avoids concrete facts, but a congruous and farseeing attitude that must amply justify him in the eyes of his contemporaries.

By 1974 there was already evidence, in the course that world events were taking, of a movement towards universalism. The Union of Soviet Socialist Republics, the European Economic Community, the efforts by the Third World, would appear to be the first steps towards what Borges has been indicating for the past fifty years. This proves both that there are definite reasons for this course to be taken and that Borges' ideas are backed by thinkers and statesmen in the rest of the world.

However, this seems to be impossible to achieve. The kind of man required for universalism could not be more contrary to our present man, devoted solely to himself and indifferent to the destiny of his fellow men. Existentialist philosophy points out this solitude to which present day man is condemned. At the same time, he is still condiitioned by territorial frontiers, racial prejudices, political trends and religious ideas, which have always

77

divided humanity. To reach universalism man must undergo a radical change. He must transcend his individualistic outlook in order to take part in the destiny of the world; he must be able to cover a wider and more complex panorama, to rise above the differences and to work for the common destiny, an eminently social man, free of hate, envy and negative reactions and capable of respecting his fellow men.

Borges tries to contribute towards the birth of this new man by means of his writing, whose object is to free us from our mental pigeon-holing and lead us to a more objective knowledge of reality. By facing the reader with the transcendental world, and the most diverse places, times and human beings, the author manages to get the reader to realize intuitively what his real dimension is within reality. By confusing him and leading him astray, he makes him doubt his own reasoning and thus destroys the cult of his personal convictions.

The sociologist, the philosopher and the psychologist all lie hidden in Borges, but instead of expressing his knowledge in a theoretical way, he prefers to apply it directly, through the possibilities his writing offers of really producing a transformation in the reader.

He has absolutely no inclination towards any country or culture. When he states that the 'gaucho' does not represent the national spirit, he is not running him down nor is he disowning him, as many people think (on the contrary, the gaucho is one of the few characters for whom he has shown a certain admiration). Borges tries to make an objective approach – without sentimental feelings for our picturesque ancestor – to the real current situation, of which he himself is a typical representative. The pseudo-nationalistic efforts to limit our present and our future to this gaucho past contradict the integration of the large number of immigrants of all classes which has taken place in the Argentine, to a degree unknown in any other country, precisely because of the characteristics of the native people.

Borges asserts in 'The Argentine Idiom and the Tradition' (*Discusión*, p. 160) 'I think that our tradition is all of the Western culture', and he points out the advantage we have of being able to handle all European subjects better than any country which is limited by a one-sided heritage. Both this approach to what is Argentine and Borges' tendency towards universalism prove that all the nations and periods that appear in his writings are not the manifestation of a cult for things foreign.

I would also like it to be clearly understood that Borges made his connection with Sufism through Spain, where Sufism co-existed with the Arab culture for eight centuries. Viewed in this way, the Orientalism in his works would cease to be an exotic and distant theme, since the author has simply retrieved, through his objectivity, a valuable part of our own Spanish heritage that was consigned to oblivion (save for the interest of a few Arabists) because of patriotic prejudices. But eight centuries of co-existence are not easily eliminated from a country's past, least of all in the case of Spain, where the Arab influence is evident in the physical aspects, the habits and the arts in general. And Sufism, precisely because it is not tied to any dogma, seems to have been one of the main factors uniting the two cultures, separated though they were by political-religious fanaticisms. Asín Palacios writes: 'But the diffusion of Sufi ideas was not limited to the Islamic sphere since, overcoming religious barriers, they influenced the philosophical life of Jewish and Christian thinkers practically from the start,' and Ana María Barrenechea writes: 'From the time of Ibn Masarra and because of him, Moslem Spain became the home of the greatest mystics.'

Borges thus shows us once again a hidden perspective of reality and probably opens the way for us to perfect our idea of the true Spanish spirit. At the same time, by bringing to life for the reader the transcendental world of intuitive knowledge, he has taken on the role that religion should assume.

In his recent book, *The Psychology of Consciousness*, the psychologist Robert Ornstein refers precisely to this aspect of religion. 'There are two major modes of consciousness in man: one is analytic, the other is holistic.... They are complementary; both have their functions. Another way to convey the dichotomy is to point to the difference between the 'rational' and the 'intuitive' sides of man. In our intellectual history we have separated these two modes of knowing into separate areas of specialization, into science and religion, for example.... With the break-up of organized religion as a major cultural force, science has become the dominant influence in our culture.' (p. 10)

Despite Borges' statements against all dogmas, he is probably closer to Jesus' real message than many orthodox Christians and his untiring investigations into the world beyond are probably the most authentic way of approaching religion for twentieth century man.

At the age of seventy and almost totally blind, Borges says a prayer which the reader feels is like a farewell and at the same time a mirror that reflects his real self:

'Thousands of times, and in the two languages that are close to me, my lips have said and will go on saying the Lord's Prayer, but only in part do I understand it. This morning, the first day of July, 1969, I want to attempt a prayer that will be my own, not handed down. I know this is an undertaking that demands an almost superhuman sincerity.... I want to be remembered less as a poet than as a friend; let someone recall a verse of Frost or of Dunbar or of the nameless Saxon who at midnight saw the shining tree that bleeds, the Cross, and let him think he heard it for the first time from my lips. The rest is of little importance; I hope oblivion will not be long in coming.... My wish is to die wholly; my wish is to die with this companion, my body.' (*Darkness*, p. 115)

Appendix

Concrete Bibliographical Data

Scattered throughout Borges' work there are extensive bibliographical data which prove beyond a doubt that Borges has probed into the Sufi literature, which until recently was quite unknown to most of us. Without making a thorough search through all his works, I am able to point out the following:

Direct References

He uses the words: Sufi, on pp. 256 and 114 of *Obra Poética* and *El Aleph* respectively; dervish, on p. 110 of *El Aleph*, pp. 138, 139 of *Cuentos Breves y Extraordinarios*, pp. 107, 110 of *Historia de la Eternidad*; theosophists, on pp. 42, 168, 174 of *Discusión*, p. 95 of *Historia de la Eternidad*, p. 33 of *El Hacedor*. He mentions the Hashishin Order on p. 109 of *Otras Inquisiciones*; the order of the Sadiyeh and Ahmediyeh on p. 183 of *Cuentos Breves y Extraordinarios*.

Further, Alicia Jurado states that when Borges was President of the Argentine Society of Writers, from 1950 to 1953, he gave lectures on 'the Sufi mystics'. (*Genio*, p. 46)

Quotations from Sufi Authors

From Sheikh Faridudin Attar: pp. 124, 125, 181 of *Discusión*, pp. 135, 143, 144, 145 of *Historia de la Eternidad*, pp. 112, 164 of *El Aleph*, p. 120 of *Otras Inquisiciones*, pp. 35, 42, 43 of *Ficciones*.

From Imam el-Ghazali: p. 91 of *El Aleph*, pp. 138, 160 of *Otras Inquisiciones*.

From Alfarabi: p. 110 of *Otras Inquisiciones*.

From Ibn el-Arabi: p. 17 of *Cuentos Breves y Extraordinarios*.

From Omar Khayyam: p. 180 Of *Obra Poética*, pp. 71, 109, 113 of *Otras Inquisiciones*, p. 60 of *El Hacedor*, pp. 73, 74 of *Elogio de la Sombra*.

From Sir Richard Burton: pp. 99, 134 of *Historia de la Enternidad*, pp. 124, 128 of *Historia de la infamia*, pp. 101, 168 of

El Aleph, p. 124 of *Evaristo Carriego,* p. 168 of *Discusión,* pp. 61, 81, 113 of *Cuentos Breves y Extraordinarios.*

From Lufi Ali Azur: i. 110 of *El Aleph.*

References to Sufi Literature

'Asrar Nama': pp. 112, 114 of *El Aleph.*

'Mantiq al-Tayr': pp. 144, 145 of *Historia de la Eternidad,* pp. 125, 181 of *Discusión,* p. 164 of *El Aleph,* p. 111 of *Otras Inquisiciones,* pp. 42, 43 of *Ficciones.*

'Tahafut-ul-falasifa': p. 91 of *El Aleph.*

'Rubaiyat': pp. 109, 113 of *Otras Inquisiciones,* pp. 73, 74 of *Elogio de la Sombra.* Referring to this book, Alicia Jurado says that Borges' father 'published the first Spanish translation of Omar Khayyam's 'Rubaiyat' and this is undoubtedly how Jorge Luís Borges became acquainted with this poet whom he admires so much.' (*Genio,* p. 27)

'The Thousand and One Nights': references to this book appear continually throughout Borges' works, even when not apparently connected with the theme (e.g. *Ficciones,* pp. 188, 190, 191). In addition Borges has made a special study of the Western translations of the book and concluded that all are without authority except Sir Richard Burton's; the latter was a member of the Sufi Qadiri Order. Borges wrote an essay on Burton as translator of the book and notes that the translation had 'one edition, limited to a thousand subscribers, members of the Burton Club, with a legal embargo on reprinting.' (*Eternidad,* p. 112) Borges proves that he owns a copy of this translation by quoting from it and by mentioning it in a bibliography. There is therefore the possibility of a direct link with Burton.

Bibliography

Barrenechea, Ana María. *Borges, the Labyrinth Maker.* New York: New York University Press, 1965. Translation by Robert Lima of *La Expresión de la Irrealidad en la Obra de Borges.* Buenos Aires: Paidós, 1967.

Borges, Jorge Luís. *The Aleph and Other Stories, 1933–1969.* London: Jonathan Cape, 1971. Translation by Norman Thomas di Giovanni of a selection of stories from:

El Aleph. Buenos Aires: Emecé, 1971.

Discusión. Buenos Aires: Emecé, 1957.

Dreamtigers. Austin: University of Texas Press, 1964. Translation by Mildred Boyer and Harold Morland of:

El Hacedor. Buenos Aires: Emecé, 1960.

Fictions. London: Calder and Boyars, 1965. Translation by Anthony Kerrigan of:

Ficciones. Buenos Aires: Emecé, 1956.

Historia de la Eternidad. Buenos Aires: Emecé, 1953.

In Praise of Darkness. London: Allen Lane, 1975. Translation by Norman Thomas di Giovanni of:

Elogio de la Sombra. Buenos Aires: Emecé, 1969.

Other Inquisitions, 1937–1952. London: Souvenir Press, 1973. Translation by Ruth L. C. Simms of:

Otras Inquisiciones. Buenos Aires: Sur, 1952.

A Personal Anthology. London: Jonathan Cape, 1968. Translation by Anthony Kerrigan of:

Antología Personal. Buenos Aires: Sur, 1961.

A Universal History of Infamy. Harmondsworth: Penguin Books, 1975. Translation by Norman Thomas di Giovanni of:

Historia Universal de la Infamia. Buenos Aires: Emecé, 1954.

Borges, Jorge Luís in collaboration with Adolfo Bioy Casares.

Cuentos Breves y Extraordinarios. Buenos Aires: Raigal, 1955.

Harss, Luís and Barbara Dohmann. *Into the Mainstream.* New

York: Harper and Row, 1966. Translation by the authors of:
Los Nuestros. Buenos Aires: Sudamericana.

Historia de la Literatura Argentina. Buenos Aires: Centro
Editor de América Latina, 1968.

Jurado, Alicia, *Genio y Figura de Jorge Luis Borges,* Editorial
Universitaria de Buenos Aires, 1966.

Ornstein, Robert E. *The Psychology of Consciousness.* San Francisco: W. H. Freeman, 1972.

Shah, Idries. *Caravan of Dreams.* London: Octagon Press, 1968.*
The Dermis Probe. London: Jonathan Cape, 1970.
The Exploits of the Incomparable Mulla Nasrudin. London:
Jonathan Cape, 1966.*
The Magic Monastery. London: Jonathan Cape, 1972.*
The Pleasantries of the Incredible Mulla Nasrudin. Lon-
don: Jonathan Cape, 1968.*
Reflections. London: Zenith Books, 1969.*
The Subtleties of the Inimitable Mulla Nasrudin. London:
Jonathan Cape, 1973.
The Sufis. New York: Doubleday, 1964.*
Tales of the Dervishes. London: Jonathan Cape, 1967.*
Thinkers of the East. London: Jonathan Cape, 1971.*
The Way of the Sufi. London: Jonathan Cape, 1968.*
Wisdom of the Idiots. London: Octagon Press, 1970.*

Sufi Classical Texts

Sheikh Faridudin Attar. *The Conference of the Birds.* Translated
by C. S. Nott. London: Routledge and Kegan Paul, 1954.

Imam el-Ghazali. *The Alchemy of Happiness.* Translated by
Claude Field. Lahore: Ashraf Press, 1964.
The Niche for Lights. Translated by W. H. T. Gairdner.
Lahore: Ashraf Press, 1952.

Shamsuddin Mohammed Hafiz, of Shiraz. *The Divan.* Translated
by Colonel Wilberforce Clarke and Mirza Bisravi. London:
Octagon Press, 1974.

Maulana Jalaludin Rumi. *Teachings of Rumi.* The Masnavi,
abridged and translated by E. H. Whinfield. London: Octagon
Press, 1973.*

Sheikh Saadi of Shiraz. *The Rose Garden.* Translated by Edward
B. Eastwick. London: Octagon Press, 1974.*

Bibliography

Hakim Sanai. *The Walled Garden of Truth.* Translated and abridged by D. L. Pendlebury. London: Octagon Press, 1974.

Mahmud Shabistari. *The Secret Garden.* Translated by Johnson Pasha. London: Octagon Press, 1969.

*Available in paperback.

Further Reading

Burke, O. M. *Among the Dervishes*. London: Octagon Press, 1973 and 1976. New York: E. P. Dutton, 1975. A Westerner's travels through the lands of the Sufis.

Fatemi, Professor N. S. *et al.*, *Sufism*, Message of Brotherhood, Harmony and Hope. South Brunswick and New York: A. S. Barnes and Company, and London: Thomas Yoseloff Ltd., 1976. Thinkers and poets of the Sufis.

Lewin, Professor L., (editor) *The Diffusion of Sufi Ideas in the West* – (1972) republished as *The Elephant in the Dark*, E. P. Dutton, 1976.

Lewin, Professor L., (editor) *The Elephant in the Dark* (Anthology of readings by and about Idries Shah and contemporary Sufism). New York: E. P. Dutton, 1976. Originally published as *The Diffusion of Sufi Ideas in the West*, by The Institute for Research on the Dissemination of Human Knowledge, 1972.

Shah, Amina *The Tale of the Four Dervishes*: London: Octagon Press, 1975. The classic by Amir Khusru, originally entitled *Bagh o Bahar* – 'Garden and Spring'.

Shah, Idries *A Veiled Gazelle* – Seeing how to See. London: Octagon Press, 1978.

Beginning to Begin – Neglected aspects of Sufi Study. London: Octagon Press, 1978. University Lectures.

The Book of the Book: London: Octagon Press, 1969. Sufi instruction-tale.

Destination Mecca, London: Octagon Press, 1957. Third Printing, illustrated, 1971. Middle Eastern journeys.

The Elephant in the Dark, London: Octagon Press, 1974. Lectures on Islam, Christianity and the Sufis given at Geneva University, 1972–73.

Learning how to Learn – 100 Conversations with Idries Shah. London: Octagon Press, 1978.

Oriental Magic, London: Rider 1956: Octagon Press, 1969,

1970, 1973. Illustrated; Foreword by Professor Louis Marin. Human minority beliefs. Chapter on Sufi organization.

Special Illumination – The Sufi use of Humour. London: Octagon Press, 1978.

Special Problems in the Study of Sufi Ideas, London: Octagon Press, 1966. Third Edition, 1974. Sussex University Seminar.

The Hundred Tales of Wisdom. London: Octagon Press, 1978.

Williams, Professor L. F. Rushbrook (editor) *Sufi Studies: East and West* A symposium of twenty-four research papers on Sufi studies. London: The Octagon Press in association with Jonathan Cape, 1973. New York: E. P. Dutton, 1974.

For further information on this
subject please write to:—

THE SOCIETY FOR SUFI STUDIES
P.O. BOX 43   LOS ALTOS
CALIFORNIA 94022   USA